with Local Tips
The author's special recommendations are highlighted in yellow throughout this guide

There are five symbols to help you find your way around this guide:

Marco Polo's top recommendations – the best in each category

sites with a scenic view

places where the local people meet

places where young people get together

(100/A1)
pages and coordinates for the Road Atlas of Normandy

This travel guide was written by Hans-Peter Reiser, who is living in the Normandy.

MARCO POLO

Travel guides and language guides in this series:

Alaska • Algarve • Amsterdam • Australia/Sydney • Bahamas • Barbados
Berlin • Brittany • California • Canada • Channel Islands • Costa Brava/
Barcelona • Costa del Sol/Granada • Côte d'Azur • Crete • Cuba • Cyprus
Dominican Republic • Eastern Canada • Eastern USA • Florence • Florida
Gran Canaria • Greek Islands/Aegean • Ibiza/Formentera • Ireland • Istanbul
Lanzarote • London • Madeira • Mallorca • Malta • Mexico • New York
New Zealand • Normandy • Paris • Prague • Rhodes • Rocky Mountains
Rome • San Francisco • Scotland • South Africa • Southwestern USA • Tenerife
Turkish Coast • Tuscany • USA: Southern States • USA: New England • Venice
Western Canada • Western USA

French • German • Italian • Spanish

Marco Polo would be very interested to hear your comments and suggestions. Please write to:

North America:
Marco Polo North America
70 Bloor Street East
Oshawa, Ontario, Canada
(B) 905-436-2525

United Kingdom:
GeoCenter International Ltd
The Viables Centre
Harrow Way
Basingstoke, Hants RG22 4BJ

Our authors have done their research very carefully, but should any errors or omissions have occurred, the publisher cannot be held responsible for any injury, damage or inconvenience suffered due to incorrect information in this guide

Cover photograph: Mont Saint Michel (Schapowalow: Huber)
Photos: Amberg (97); Archiv für Kunst und Geschichte Berlin (16); author (14, 30, 44, 48, 50, 61, 64, 75, 82, 86, 94); bildarchiv steffens: Bauer (43); Frei (7, 11, 23, 29, 35, 40, 56, 58, 67, 68, 72, 76); Friedrichsmeier (8, 18, 24, 26); Kallabis (4); Lange (20); Mauritius: Hubatka (99), Schuster (39); Thomas (49, 52)

2nd revised edition 2000
© Mairs Geographischer Verlag, Ostfildern, Germany
Translator: Heather Stacey
English edition 2000: Gaia Text, Munich
Editorial director: Ferdinand Ranft
Chief editor: Marion Zorn
Cartography for the Road Atlas: © Mairs Geographischer Verlag
Design and layout: Thienhaus/Wippermann
Printed in Germany

All rights reserved. No part of this publication may be reproduced or transmitted in any form or by any means, electronic or mechanical including photocopying, recording or by any information storage and retrieval systems without prior permission from the publisher

CONTENTS

Discover Normandy!

Lively and cheerful on the coast and quiet and dreamy inland

Anyone who is not familiar with Normandy and who attempts to build up a picture of the area by looking at a map might easily be inclined to conjure up an image of Normandy as an extensive and inviting coastal landscape. This image is simultaneously picturesque and captivating, combining wild breakers crashing on the steep, deeply fissured cliffs with the calm swell of waves breaking gently on fine, sandy bathing beaches. Above, scraps of cloud blown about by the wind add white blotches to the bright blue of the sky. The image is completed by scenes of carefree days spent on the beach, little fishing boats quietly bobbing up and down out on the water and gulls screeching as they swoop through the air. It is no surprise that a map of the coastline along the English Channel should create such an apparently pleasant impression. Normandy – a bathing paradise? Actually, this perception is by no means incorrect.

Magnificent natural scenery: the Porte and Aiguille d'Aval near Etretat

Those who already know something about this area will go a bit further inland and will combine the image of this part of the coast with idyllic impressions, first of wind-blown hedges, shrubs and bushes, then of lush green meadows, trees covered in apple blossom and fields as far as the eye can see. In between there are cows and sheep dozing gently in fertile pasture land. Normandy – a beautiful garden? This image is also correct.

Those who are already a little more familiar with Normandy will realise that these descriptions are still not exhaustive. To complete the picture of the region it is necessary to go much further inland, with its hills and ravines, its woods and forests, its rivers and trees. Normandy – a splendid natural landscape? This notion really captures the real character of this wonderful area best of all.

Thus, visitors who come to Normandy brimming with curiosity and anticipation will find a natural environment which, in every aspect, is as pure, unspoilt and delightful as the ever-popular *cidre*, Normandy's famous apple drink.

Back to the coast. The stretch of coastline which belongs to Normandy begins at Le Tréport and extends along the *Côte d'Albâtre* (Alabaster Coast) as far as Etretat. The sheer, brilliant-white cliffs, which have been formed at the edge of the chalk plateau of the *Pays de Caux*, sometimes reach exhilarating heights of 200 m. And the tireless ebb and flow of the waves means that the crumbling of the chalk continues without end. This is how the rock formations have been created which are part of Normandy's unique natural features. The fantastic *Aiguille,* the famous needle-shaped rock near Etretat alone, makes a trip worthwhile. But it is not just for the sights that visitors come to this region, they also flock here to relax and bathe. And nature has provided the perfect environment for this. Over the course of thousands of years, the rivers which flow through the plateau have carved out beautiful valleys, at the end of which densely-populated harbour cities, such as Dieppe, have grown up, as well as cosy little fishing villages like Le Tréport and, increasingly, charming seaside resorts like Fécamp and Veulettes-sur-Mer. The route to this lively coastal region wends its way through the quiet *Pays de Caux* and the adjoining *Pays de Bray*, further inland, which provide good land for arable and cattle farming. The smell of agriculture is heavy in the air in many places. So it is with real pleasure that visitors detect the unique aroma of the cider-bottling plants near Longueville and the equally characteristic scent of the cheese dairies at Neufchâtel-en-Bray.

The chalk plateau comes to an end on its western side in the wide *Val de Seine.* The gentle gradient here causes the river to loop and wind. However, this fact did not prevent the Seine from being of great historical significance and a constant bone of contention for Normandy. Nor did it prevent the river from becoming (and remaining) the most important transport and trade route in northern France. In the loops of the river, many towns, villages and industries have sprung up, making their living from the river. Yet even long miles of manufacturing complexes cannot hide the fact that the Seine flows through an extraordinarily interesting and idyllic valley. On its way to the sea the river passes some impressive natural features, such as the great bow at Les Andelys. It winds through towns with unparalleled historic monuments, such as Rouen, and its rippling progress provides a gentle contrast to the peace and quiet of monasteries and abbeys. Its banks are lined with great tracts of forest, such as the *Forêt de Brotonne.* Finally, the Seine estuary spreads out in the *Baie de la Seine*, at Le Havre, on the edge of the Département of *Seine-Maritime.*

Probably the most attractive section of the Seine belongs to the adjoining Département of *Eure*, to the south. It begins at the little village of Giverny, which provided the Impressionist painter Claude Monet with a refuge in an enchanting landscape, and extends as far as Les Andelys where, high above a loop of the Seine, Richard the Lionheart built the *Château Gaillard* during his 12th-century campaign against the French King Philippe-Auguste.

At the heart of the *Pays d'Ouche* which extends to the west of the Seine is the historically important town of Evreux. It is not only to its fine cathedral that the town owes its importance – Evreux developed over the centuries to become the central focus of an area which has succeeded in retaining the tranquil, Norman character of its past. Beyond Evreux, delightful pastoral landscapes, streches of fields and large tracts of woodland extend northwards, bordering the lovely *Parc Naturel Régional de Brotonne,* until the coast is reached. At the *Côte de Grâce,* the Département meets the bustling activity of the lively tourist resorts.

Briefly interrupted by the *Côte de Grâce,* a coastal region with cliffs reaching as high as 100 m, the Département of *Calvados* begins at the pretty town of Honfleur. With its brilliant *Côte Fleurie* this is certainly one of its highlights. The elegant bathing resorts of Deauville and Trouville draw streams of visitors like bees to a honey pot so that, in the busy high season it is no easy feat to press your way through the tu-

Cabourg: beach life à la Normandie

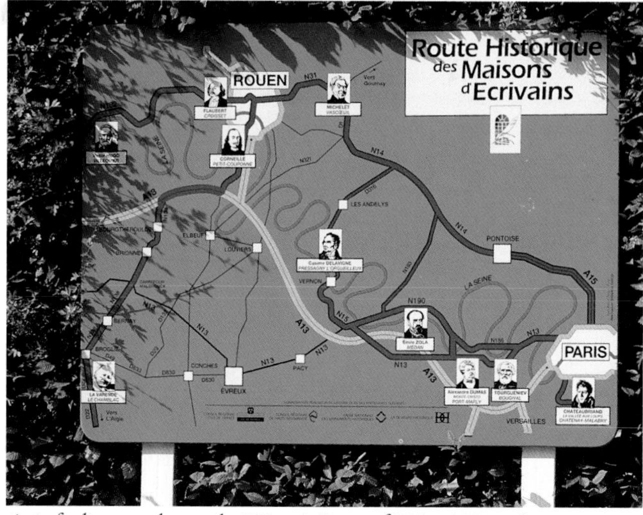

A tip for literature lovers: the "Historic Route of Writers' Houses"

mult to one of the overcrowded social events, let alone to visit one of the tourist attractions. Further along the coast are a series of bathing resorts which run into one another and are actually much friendlier and more bearable for those who dislike crowds. This is especially true of the places on the *Côte de Nacre* with their long, sandy and pebbly beaches.

The *Plage de Débarquement*, as the western section of the *Côte de Nacre* has been known since the dramatic landing here by the Allies on 6 June 1944, evokes very emotive images which are not only linked with the landing places on *Omaha Beach* and *Utah Beach*, but which apply to the whole of Normandy. The climactic capture of the beaches came in the wake of bitter fighting on practically every metre of Norman soil. There is not a town, not a village here which did not have to endure terrible times and suffer the most appalling destruction. It was only after two months, with the capture of Rouen, that Normandy was finally liberated and a major step was taken towards the end of World War II and deliverance from horror and suffering. Countless cemeteries, memorials and museums keep the memory of those fateful events alive – they are here as a constant reminder and an eternal warning.

Inland from the coast lie the flat, seemingly endless plains of the *Pays d'Auge* and the *Bessin*, which are used for agriculture, particularly for growing wheat. The cows which graze the lush pasture land with such obvious enjoyment provide the cheese used to make Camembert and Livarot cheeses. The fruit trees which bloom in the luxuriant orchards provide the apples for cider and calvados. The region's three famous "Cs" should rightly be mentioned in any introduction.

Highlights of a different kind characterise the historic towns of Bayeux, Caen and Lisieux with their wonderful religious buildings. Together with all the other places of interest in this Département which is so rich in beauty, they complete the picture of a unique landscape.

The route all round the perimeter of the Département *Manche*, the western part of the region, just begs to be explored. Setting off eastwards, the drive along the coast takes in the two north-west corners of the region, the *Pointe de Barfleur* and the *Cap de la Hague*, and then finally leads down to the legendary monastery in the *Baie du Mont Saint Michel*. It is a unique route, combining cliffs buffeted by waves, fine sandy bathing beaches and a wide selection of major historical buildings. However, it is easy to miss the extraordinarily interesting countryside inland. It is a wind-lashed and consequently barren landscape, but in early and late summer it is transformed into colourful, blooming heathland. The *Cotentin* peninsula is a delight in itself and all in all the *Manche* is an exhilerating and fascinating area to visit.

While those who come here for a beach holiday usually prefer to keep to the fine sandy beaches and the foaming waves, those who are more interested in the unspoilt natural landscape favour *Orne*. This quiet, peaceful Département shares the area in the north known as *Suisse Normande* with *Calvados* and in the south, the *Parc Naturel Régional Normandie-Maine* is shared with neighbouring *Maine*. In between them is *Perche*, which connects the two areas, turning the region into an individual entity with its own character. There are hills and valleys, woods and meadows, hedgerows and bushy areas – ideal for walking, horse-riding and cycle tours. *Orne* is so much more than a simple stopping-off place on the way to the coast or to one of the neighbouring regions – for those who enjoy it, it is the perfect place to experience and delight in pure nature.

Even a casual look at this brief overview of the features of the five Départements produces a picture of Normandy as an extraordinarily attractive natural landscape. To complement the rather poetic picture already drawn, it is worth including some more prosaic details here with a number of statistics. The region is divided into Haute-Normandie *(Eure, Seine-Maritime)*, with an area of 12,258 sq km and Rouen as its capital, and Basse-Normandie *(Calvados, Manche, Orne)* with an area of 17,583 sq km and Caen as its capital. Normandy has a total area of 29,841 sq km and a population of around 3.2 million.

Yet Normandy is not simply an attractive combination of lively coastal areas, endless plains and peaceful inland regions. Normandy is a land which is alive with centuries of history and enriched by its architecture, its art and its culture. The importance of the contribution which Normandy has made both to France and to Europe as a whole is immense and immeasurable.

A good way not only to discover the beauty of Normandy's natural landscape and explore its historical attractions, but also to become better acquainted with the region and gain a more profound impression of it, is to go on one of the well-devised history trails which guide visitors through the extensive, varied and often hidden cultural heritage of the region. They also have the great advantage that they not only link individual sites together to form one interesting trail, but that the route from one place to the next is well-signposted. More detailed information is available from any tourist office.

One lovely example is the *Route du Val de Seine et des Abbayes,* the famous Seine Valley and Abbey Route. It goes through the richly varied section of the Seine valley, which runs from Rouen to Le Havre and passes chalk cliffs, grassy slopes and woods. The route starts in Rouen at the *Abbaye Saint-Ouen,* goes on to Saint-Martin-de-Boscherville to the *Abbaye Saint-Georges* and then comes to the lovely *Abbaye Jumièges* and the *Abbaye Saint-Wandrille.* After this it goes through Gruchet-le-Valasse, taking in the *Abbaye Valasse,* and finally ending up in Montivilliers with the *Abbaye Saint-Saveur.* This trail offers some impressive insights and definitely whets the appetite for more. And Normandy can serve up plenty more of these architectural delights with their turrets and spires, as the region is rich in splendid monasteries, most of which were founded in the 11th century. Examples include the *Abbaye aux Hommes* in Caen, the *Abbaye Saint-Trinité* in Lessay, the *Abbaye Notre-Dame-de-Bernay,* which is the oldest religious building known in Normandy, the Cistercian abbey of Mortemer, and many more. However, last but by no means least, the crowning glory of monastic splendour is naturally the holy rock of *Mont Saint Michel.* Other high points of religious architecture are the region's many cathedrals. They are not only impressive for the aesthetics of their architecture, but are also fascinating for what they tell us about mediaeval building styles. A few examples might include the Early Gothic pointed arches of Lisieux, the Gothic double-towered façade, high nave and lantern tower above the transept, found in Evreux, Rouen, Bayeux, Coutances and Fécamp, and finally the Flamboyant style of the Late Gothic and Early Renaissance found in the church at Verneuil-sur-Arve. These sacred buildings belong to the treasures of Normandy.

Another popular tour is the *Route Normandie–Vexin,* which takes visitors to some beautiful châteaux, as well as monasteries (the Cistercian abbey of Fontaine-Guérard, the Abbey at Mortemer and the church at Vernon), museums (the Archaeological Museum at Guiry-en-Vexin) and gardens (Giverny). The route also includes Rouen and Lyons-la-Fôret, since they are so full of interesting buildings and sights. However, the main focus of the route is the châteaux at Martainville, Vascœuil, Gisors, Boury, Ambleville, Gaillard-Les-Andelys and Bizy. Normandy boasts an extraordinary number of castles and fortresses. This is

Flamboyant architecture at its best: the cathedral of Notre-Dame in Rouen

due to the fact that the Normans were embroiled in so many wars and violent clashes during the course of the Middle Ages. Originally the Normans built castles designed as well-fortified defensive strongholds, with a square (later round) *donjon* forming the central structure. Once the country had become more peaceable, a new phase began with the building of the Norman *manoirs*, which combined living and working quarters in a fortified complex. These were no longer merely functional buildings and so appearance became more important. This led to the use of half-timbering and tiles and rich colours and patterns. These attractive early feudal residences gradually developed into the châteaux. Many châteaux were built in the Italian Renaissance style with intricate plans and elaborate façades. Good examples of these are the *Château d'O* and *Fontaine-Henry*. The splendid palaces in the towns of Evreux (the Bishop's Palace) and Rouen (Palace of Justice) were built in this style and were also designed to show off the wealth and power of the nobility. After the religious wars there was a second wave of building, during which the huge Baroque châteaux with their strictly symmetrical architecture were erected. An important element of these châteaux was the gardens which were also strictly geometrical, designed in the French style. Examples are the *Château Balleroy* and the *Château Cany*. The next development in architectural style was Classicism which brought with it a much simpler, rectilinear approach and gardens and parks in the English style. One example of this is the *Château Sassy* with its extensive, seemingly untouched garden.

The *Route Historique des Maisons d'Écrivains*, takes visitors to the houses of famous writers. It passes through stretches of idyllic countryside which attracted so many writers and also extends into the neighbouring region of the *Ile de France*. From the Seine in

Paris to Rouen and beyond, the route offers literature-lovers an impressive tour. Sites along the way include the houses which were lived in or visited by François Châteaubriand, Alexandre Dumas, Gustave Flaubert, Victor Hugo, Emile Zola and others. The tradition of writing in Normandy dates back to the Middle Ages and the monks who lived in the abbeys here. They worked conscientiously to produce historical writings in Latin, in which they glorified the deeds of the Norman dukes. They were followed by early historians, such as Ordericus Vitalis and Robert of Torigni. Centuries later Norman philosophers and writers concerned themselves with the intellectual ideas of the time. For example, after spending some time in America, Alexis de Tocqueville wrote his book, *Démocratie en Amérique*, a very perceptive description of the opportunities and future for democratic social structures. Other writers whose houses may be visited on this trail include Jules Barbey d'Aurevilly and Marcel Proust, who came here every year to spend his holidays in Cabourg.

As well as attracting writers, Normandy has also always been very popular with artists. At long last there is now also a separate trail devoted to painters. They certainly earned it, for the often described, soft atmospheric light and the unique features of the Normandy coastline held a magical attraction for large numbers of painters, many of whom later became famous. The first to come under the spell of this magical region was Nicolas Poussin in the 17th century. Two hundred years later artists started to flock here. The white cliffs in Etretat captivated Gustave Courbet and Eugène Boudin was fascinated by the little harbour at Honfleur. Many other artists came to join them and so the "Honfleur School" was founded, with Claude Monet, Jean-Frédéric Bazille, Alfred Sisley and many more. They developed the Impressionist style of painting which was based on a new technique, whereby colours were applied separately onto the canvas. Claude Monet became a master of this technique and moved into his refuge in Giverny which can still be seen today. The artists' communities remained here for a long time, particularly as the painters developed new styles based on a continued fascination with the magic of the coast of Normandy. This was certainly true in the case of Georges Seurat, Raoul Dufy and Georges Braque who is buried in the cemetery at Varengeville.

And so back to the holiday trails which are so numerous that they cannot all be mentioned. There is the "Ivory and Spice Trail", the historic "Dukes' Trail", the "Glass-blowers' Trail" and others with similarly exotic-sounding names. One more route however should be picked out here: the "Stud Farm and Château Trail". This leads through *Orne*, taking in a series of majestic châteaux and equally fine stud farms, such as the *Haras National du Pin.* And the horses, which are a beautiful and universal feature of the entire region, also provide the final proof that Normandy is indeed a natural wonder.

History at a glance

3000 BC
First settlements are established

1000 BC
The Celts settle in Normandy

56 BC
Caesar conquers Gaul. First Roman settlements at Caen, Coutances, Lisieux and Rouen

2nd century AD
Christianity begins to spread. Rouen is the first diocesan town

486
The Merovingian king, Clovis, defeats the Romans at Soissons

6th /7th century
A large number of churches and monasteries are founded. In 709 Mont Saint Michel is constructed

841
The Vikings attack Normandy. Plundering and destruction in the towns and in the countryside

911
The treaty of Saint-Clair-sur-Êpte grants the Vikings the right to settle. Their leader, Rollo, is made first Duke of Normandy

1066
William the Conqueror wins the Battle of Hastings and becomes King of England. The Anglo-Norman kingdom is a threat to the French monarchy

1196
Richard the Lionheart builds Château Gaillard to defend Normandy against France

1204
The Anglo-Norman kingdom disintegrates and becomes a French province

1340
Hundred Years' War between France and England

1431
Joan of Arc is burnt at the stake in Rouen

1486
Normandy finally falls and is absorbed permanently into France

1639
Tax increases lead to a revolt which is crushed by Cardinal Richelieu

1806
The Continental System imposed by Napoleon against England has a devastating effect on Norman shipping

1920
The Vatican canonises Joan of Arc

1940–44
Occupation of Normandy by German troops. 1942 brings the first liberation attempts by the Allies at Dieppe

1944
D-Day landings on the coast of Normandy. Many towns are destroyed

1974
Mont Saint Michel is classified as an historic monument

Le Tricorne

From Camembert to the trou normand

Everything you should know about Normandy

Camembert

When Normandy is mentioned, the first thing that springs to mind for the gourmet are the "Three Cs" – Camembert, Calvados and Cidre. It is well known that Normandy is a region for connoisseurs but at the forefront is the famous soft cheese from the *Pays d'Auge* which has become a symbol of good taste, both within France and abroad. As Camembert began to make its triumphal advance around the world, it was quickly copied – not least because its unpatented name could be used by anyone who chose to do so. The original cheese, now recognised by the V.C.N. (Véritable Camembert Normand) mark, comes from the cheese-making centre of Vimoutiers. Just four kilometres away is the little village of Camembert where the cheese was "invented". Legend has it that there was a priest who fled here during the French Revolution and was sheltered by a Madame Marie Harel. In gratitude he is said to have given her the recipe for his creation. Madame Harel passed it on to her daughter of the same name who was quite business-minded and began to market the delicacy packed in straw. She found support for this in the person of Napoleon III who came to appreciate the new dairy delicacy during his journey to Argentan and was responsible for it becoming acceptable at court. The only thing standing in the way of major success was the perishability of the cheese. However, this was solved by Monsieur Auguste Lepetit who developed the now famous wooden box. Today over thirty million Camemberts are produced every year and sold world-wide.

It's hard to drag yourself away from the charming town of Etretat with its elegant half-timbered buildings

Half-timbering

There is something fascinating about half-timbered houses wherever they are. They exude an atmosphere of tradition, of being long-established and somehow safe. There is scarcely anyone who wouldn't like to live in one of these lovely houses. And there is scarcely anyone who, on seeing a half-timbered house, does not reach straight away for the camera to capture the enchanting image on film. The houses are truly a feast for the eyes and Normandy is a great place to see them. Almost every town and village boasts *colombages*, as they are called in French, in plenty. They are built in the traditional Norman style, characterised by long, high beams parallel to one another, with beautiful herringbone patterns or diagonal crosses in between. The Norman half-timbered buildings are always black or brown and white, but it is still worth taking coloured photos, as the obligatory flowers make a lovely splash of colour.

Flamboyant

Those interested in the history of art have a wonderful time in Normandy. This is largely due to the amazing architecture of many of the buildings here. There is a wealth of different styles both in the towns and in the countryside. Norman architecture is particularly characterised by the exciting Flamboyant interpretations of the Late Gothic period. At the end of the 15th century, while architects elsewhere were beginning to embrace the Renaissance, in Normandy they remained loyal to the Flamboyant until well after the Hundred Years' War. The style is expressed through dainty filigree ornamentation. Impressive examples can be seen in the "Butter Tower" of Rouen Cathedral and the decoration of Evreux Cathedral.

Invasion

With the failure of the commando operation in Dieppe in August 1942 which involved 5,000 men, the Allies discovered at terrible cost that it would not be possible to take the German lines of defence by surprise. The attempt to capture the harbour and to create a bridgehead cost the Allies 3,350 casualties and prisoners.

Two years later, *Operation Overlord* was planned right down to the last detail and painstakingly prepared. The decision was made to break through the Atlantic

D-Day, 6 June 1944, the Allies landing in Normandy

Wall along the flat beaches of the *Côte de Nacre* and the *Cotentin* peninsula with all force. And that is what happened. Delayed by a day because of poor weather conditions, in the early hours of 6 June 1944, the storming of the *Plages du Débarquement* finally took place. There was little the Germans could do against the combined forces of the Allies who, with nearly 7,000 ships and landing craft, ferried across over 136,000 men. Nevertheless, there still followed a whole series of bitter battles which culminated in the terrible battle of the Falaise Pocket. It was only when Rouen was eventually captured on 30 August 1944 that the occupation of Normandy was finally over. However, the cost of liberation was high. Nearly 100,000 people, including 37,000 Allies lost their lives. Most of the towns and villages had been almost completely destroyed. There are many military cemeteries and countless ruined bunkers which bear witness today to Normandy's "Longest Day".

Joan of Arc

Among France's many incredible historical figures, one extraordinary young girl from the the countryside must surely rank among the foremost. Here the "Maid of Orleans" still holds her ground as patron saint of France today. Her short life was full of symbolism and drama. As a child she lived through the terrifying events of the Hundred Years' War. The bitter power struggle between France and England as they fought over the French crown left the country steeped in fear and misery. After 1415, as the English King Henry V gradually captured the country, region by region, until even Paris was under his control, the final outcome of the war appeared to be a foregone conclusion. However, 1429 brought the finest hour of the "Maid of Orleans" and a decisive turning point was reached.

Joan of Arc was born in 1412 in Domrémy-la-Pucelles in Lorraine, the daughter of a seemingly wealthy farmer. As a young girl Joan believed herself to be called "by divine voices" to liberate her country from the English. After an initial failed attempt, she succeeded the second time in convincing the Dauphin at the royal court in Chinon of her divine mission. In 1429, at the head of an army of 3,000 men, she liberated the town of Orléans which had been besieged by the English and succeeded in making a significant breakthrough with an amazing victory at Patay. On 16 July 1429, Charles VII was crowned King of France in Reims. During the period which followed, as the French attempted to drive the English out of the country once and for all, Joan of Arc was taken prisoner on 23 May 1430 by the Burgundians who were fighting on the opposing side and was handed over to the arch enemy, the English. They set up a tribunal of bishops and abbots in Rouen. Under the presidency of Pierre Cauchon, later Bishop of Lisieux, Joan was found guilty of witchcraft and heresy and on 30 May 1431 she was burnt at the stake in the *Place du Vieux-Marché*. From Charles VII for whom she had smoothed the way to the throne, there came no help. It was only twenty years after-

Joan of Arc, victorious over the English: statue in Pennedepie

wards, when he captured Rouen, that he repealed the verdict. In 1920 Joan of Arc was canonised by the Vatican.

Claude Monet

In the middle of the 19th century, the soft, ever-changing light of Normandy drew many young artists to the coast. Honfleur and Etretat, with their spectacular natural features, soon became artists' colonies. Eugène Boudin set up the "Honfleur School" in his native town and stimulated the work of the Impressionists who were to revolutionise European painting. Under his influence, Claude Monet, who was born in Paris in 1840, became one of the protagonists of the new style. There are countless magnificent and now priceless paintings which bear witness to his genius and creativity. In 1881 he moved from Honfleur to rural Giverny and created his magical, uniquely idyllic garden which provided the subject for many of his pictures. Claude Monet died in 1926 and is buried in the cemetery at Giverny.

Lace-making

The artistic threadwork created around the needles of the lace cushion is a technique which was developed in Flanders. Brussels lace was surpassed by lace creations from Venice which fetched incredibly high prices. In order to stem the flow of money which was spent on these works of art which were, of course, highly prized at the French court, a royal decree was published in 1665 ordering lace to be made in Alençon. Very soon the French lace developed its own unique style; decorative motifs with strong outlines which were sewn onto a fine, hand-made net. The swift and long-lasting success of the Norman lace was due to the beautiful lace design known as the Point d'Alençon which was developed by Madame La Perrière. In the 19th century lace began to be manufactured using machines and this started to supersede the sumptuous hand-made items. A well-deserved tribute is paid to the art of lace-making in the museums in Alençon and Argentan.

Normans

They came over the sea from the North and invaded the country again and again, stealing whatever they could lay their hands on. It was not only Normandy which was subject to the terrible raids of the Danes, Norwegians and the Vikings. They raped and pillaged whole tracts of the countryside so that large areas of Europe trembled at the mention of their names. However, they had a particular liking for this region which, with its coast and rivers, was the perfect target for their tactics. They appeared in small, manoeuvrable ships, spreading fear before them, stole everything they could find and then disappeared as quickly as they had arrived. Nowhere was safe from them, neither monasteries and abbeys nor towns and villages. In the course of time, the raids became fewer and, as the Vikings began to tire of always being on the move, they started to settle here. However, they then became victims themselves of their advancing compatriots. They had to defend themselves and by the beginning of the 10th century, under the leadership of Rollo, they had become a powerful force. The Franconian King Charles le Simple, was shrewd enough to accept the new balance of power. In 911 he signed the Treaty of Saint-Clair-sur-Êpte with the Norman ruler, granting the invaders right of settlement in the wide area around the Seine. Rollo was baptised and became Robert, first Duke of Normandy. This marked the birth of a land which henceforth knew no rest and began to flourish.

Tapestry

The invasion of 1944 is omnipresent, not only in the people's memories. There are enormous archives of authentic film and photographic documentation. Thus, it is easy to forget that for centuries before 1944 there had already been countless spectacular invasions on both sides of the Channel. However, one of the earliest of these is also well-documented pictorially. This was the crossing over to and conquering of England by William, then Duke or Normandy. On a strip of linen which is 70 m long and 50 cm wide, 58 different embroidered pictures portray the events of 900 years ago just as clearly and vividly as a modern *bande dessinée,* or cartoon strip. The great attraction of Bayeux hangs in the *Centre Guillaume le Conquérant* which is housed in a converted former Jesuit College, and remains unceasingly popular with crowds of visitors. The exhibition begins in the entrance hall with videos and charts which provide background information about the tapestry. An audio-visual commentary then takes visitors through the individual scenes of the tapestry so that no details are missed.

trou normand

It is well known that Calvados is held in great esteem in Normandy. It is an extremely popular liquor which is often drunk as an undoubtedly effective *digestif,* the crowning glory at the end of an exquisite meal. However, it is also often drunk as the *trou normand,* the "Norman Hole" – knocked back straight, between courses, in order to create a sufficient "hole" or "gap" for the next course. This becomes very expensive if you order a meal with lots of courses!

A feast à la normande

From "bon appétit" to "à votre santé" – the culinary delights of Norman cuisine are worthy of praise indeed

Even at the time when the highly-prized French cuisine was rightly trying to make radical changes, Norman cuisine remained true to itself. *La nouvelle cuisine* tried in vain to influence the culinary habits and preferences if the tradition-conscious Normans. And this is a just as well. After all, who would actually want to miss out on the diverse recipes and delicious ingredients of eating *à la normande*? Not the locals anyway and certainly not the visitors who look forward to sampling the local cuisine. However, be warned: the food in Normandy tends to be rather rich and hearty. For example, a delicious *sauce normande* is also dangerously laden with calories. However, food in Normandy is simply unthinkable without butter, cream and especially *crème fraîche.* The irresistibly ennobling calvados also forms an essential part of the meal. There's nothing for it but to banish any reservations and tuck in.

In first place must be les fruits de mer

So, let's see what there is to whet your appetite. The obvious starting point is the diverse range of seafood delicacies which are to be found in this part of the world. Freshly caught fish and seafood play a dominant role in the dishes to be found on the menu in most restaurants in Normandy. There are plenty of different examples. What about *fruits de mer* for instance? Oysters, shrimps, crayfish, mussels, crabs and more besides are all served in a colourful mêlée, some raw, some cooked. Or you might choose *huîtres*, oysters, with a sauce of shallots and wine vinegar. Then there are the little *demoiselles de Cherbourg,* small lobsters cooked in a wine stock and served in butter. Another dish is *marmite dieppoise*, a delicious fish stew made with lots of different sorts of fish, mussels, shrimps, vegetables, butter and a hefty dollop of cream. Mussel dishes are both traditional and popular. For example, *moules marinières,* steamed mussels with shallots, parsley and butter, or *moules bernevalaise,* which are steamed in a *cidre* sauce with shallots. Further inland, freshwater fish are very popular. The rivers and lakes teem with all the fish the pampered gourmet could wish for. Anyone with a weakness for a finely-cooked trout is in the right place here. In Normandy the trout is steamed and served with a delicate sauce, usually flavoured with calvados. Trout is also served *à la dieppoise* which includes the addition of boiled shrimps and mussels. Another popular fish is sole, which is delicious, for example when served with mussels, shrimps, onions, vegetables, eggs, cream and herbs. Just have a look at the menu, order what you fancy and then sit back and enjoy the culinary creativity of Normandy's cuisine.

The king of all meat dishes must surely be *canard à la rouennaise,* roast duck with a sauce made from duck's blood, red wine and a generous shot of calvados. Lamb *pré-salé* is also a delicious local speciality. The salt plains around the *Baie du Mont Saint Michel* provide a habitat for aromatic herbs which imbue the meat with its own unique, unmistakable flavour. One appetising example is *gigot,* a leg of mutton which is roasted in the Granville style in a *cidre* and cream sauce.

Other famous specialities include good honest sausages. The *boudin noir* must top any list. This is a black pudding from Mortagne-au-Perche which is mouth-wateringly spicy and is often served with fried onions on a bed of apple rings. Its counterpart is *boudin blanc,* white pudding, made from chicken or veal with eggs and cream. Very popular and more expensive is the spicy *andouillette,* a delicate sausage wrapped in the skin of pig's bladder. The *andouille* is another sausage speciality which comes from Vire and is made from calf and pig offal.

Other specialities include the wafer-thin *crêpes,* which are served with a wide variety of different delicious fillings. Each *crêperie* offers its own specially-created fillings of which they are always justifiably proud. Just ask for the most highly recommended filling and sit back and enjoy!

It is no surprise that Normandy, which boasts over thirty different sorts of cheese, is known as *la région des fromages.* First and foremost is the legendary *Camembert,* the little round of soft cheese which is only the genuine article if it bears the mark V.C.N. Then there is the spicy *Livarot* with its red rind, which is runny when

A question of taste

Pré-salé is a word which makes the heart of a real gourmet beat faster. It is a word which conjures up an image of the cows and sheep which are grazed on the lush pasture land of the increasingly silted-up Baie du Mont Saint Michel. The grass which grows here is imbued with a particular aroma which comes from the high salt content of the meadows and this aroma gives the meat the unique flavour which so many find irresistible. *Pré-salé* can be sampled in every good restaurant.

cut. Another mouth-watering delicacy is *Neufchâtel* from the Pays de Bray which is mild and creamy beneath its mouldy rind. One of the most popular cheeses, partly because of the price, is the square *Pont l'Evêque.* Beneath the yellow rind is a cheese which just melts in the mouth.

So all that remains is the last course, the dessert. As the people of Normandy tend to be sweet-toothed, the choice is tempting and extensive. Here are just three examples. *Douillons,* are pears encased in pastry. Then there are *bourdelots,* apples in puff pastry stuffed with butter, sugar and cinnamon. Finally there is the *tarte aux pommes,* an apple pie with a wonderfully thin pastry and *crème fraîche,* which is served flambéed with calvados. This must surely be the crowning glory of the *menu à la normande. Bon appétit!*

Naturally, delights such as these should not be sampled without something to drink. Normandy does not produce its own wine. However *cidre,* delicious, effervescent fermented apple juice can be always be ordered in every good restaurant. For this is definitely the best and most palatable accompaniment to every meal in Normandy. Sweet, semi-dry and dry varieties are available. *Cidre fermier,* which comes in a champagne bottle has the highest alcohol content and is of particularly high quality, although it is naturally more expensive. Incidentally *poiré,* similar to cidre but made from pears, is popular both in the region and beyond and many prefer it to cider – so be sure to try it.

A special treat, not just for connoisseurs, is *calvados,* known affectionately as *calva.* This is a delectable apple spirit which is drunk at every opportunity – before, during and after the meal. Its quality is gauged according to age. It ranges from three stars (two years old) to *Réserve* (three years old) and VS OP or *Grande Réserve* (five years old). *Très Vieille Réserve* (six years and over) is the highest quality. The best varieties come from the *Pays d'Auge.* Because it is distilled twice it is entitled to be labelled AOC.

A mixture of herbs used to make the famous liqueur "Bénédictine"

The most popular aperitifs are *pommereau* (2/3 cidre and 1/3 Calvados) and *Bénédictine,* a liqueur which is distilled with great care by the monks at the monastery at Fécamp. *À votre santé!*

Antie
St Maclou

Camembert, Calvados and Cidre

Normandy loves its treats and delicacies and shares them generously with all who come here

While shopping is usually a fairly stressful activity, a relaxed holiday atmosphere transforms it into a positively enjoyable experience. This is especially true in Normandy where the range of products is incredibly wide. Particularly popular items to take back home are the many delicacies from land and sea. Anyone who fancies treating themselves will enjoy rummaging in boutiques and dusty second-hand book shops.

There are no strictly official opening hours. Most shops are open from 8.30 am until 12.30 pm and in the afternoons from 2 pm until 7 or 7.30 pm. The supermarkets are open the whole day and also on Sunday mornings but are closed all day on Mondays. The way the different opening hours are arranged means that there is always a shop open somewhere so visitors need not worry about running out of anything.

The choice of marvellous souvenirs is endless: antiques, hand-made lace, copper kitchenware and much more

The best thing about Normandy is the weekly market. Almost every town and village has a fixed market day of which it is justly proud. It is a really enjoyable experience to stroll between the stands which overflow with farm produce and delicacies from the sea. No-one can resist making a purchase for long. The local market traders love to have a bit of a chat, even if the language barrier can make conversation a little stilted.

The options for souvenirs are many and varied; cheeses packed in wooden boxes *cidre, calva* or the famous *Bénédictine* liqueur. The sweet-toothed among those back home will enjoy treats such as *sucre de pomme,* caramelised apple sweets.

If you want to spend a bit more then you might decide to buy one of the wonderful copper kitchenware items from Villedieu-les-Poêles, exquisite lace articles from Alençon and Argentan and the famous faïences from Rouen. In addition, there are plenty of *marchands d'antiquités* in Normandy, where an exciting discovery could make your suitcase heavier and your purse lighter.

Artisanal
Normandie
Artisanal
Normandie
Petit
Artisanal
Normandie

Festivals for all

The people of Normandy certainly know how to celebrate and visitors are welcome to join in

As is the case throughout France, there is not a town or village in Normandy which does not find the opportunity to celebrate a lively and eventful festival at least once a year. Most of these are based on traditional festivals which bring the people together for a convivial celebration. In addition, religious, public and patriotic festivals are also very popular. For instance, Bastille Day on 14 July is the high point of the year in every region. Whether it is horse racing in Deauville, the music festival in Honfleur, the pilgrimage to Mont Saint Michel or the black pudding festival in Mortagne-au-Perche, locals and visitors participate with heart and soul. They are all wonderful opportunities to observe and become acquainted with the people and the customs of the region. So it is well worth going to the local tourist information bureau on your arrival to find out about when and where the festivals take place. Then you can go along and join in. If you want to make friends, then naturally the best way to do so is to embrace the local culture.

Culinary delights are everywhere: oysters and cider from Rouen

PUBLIC HOLIDAYS

1 January
Easter Monday
1 May
8 May *(commemorating the end of World War II)*
Ascension Day; Whit Monday
★ 14 July *(Bastille Day)*
15 August *(Assumption Day)*
1 November *(All Saints' Day)*
11 November *(Armistice Day, end of World War I)*
25 December *(Christmas Day)*

FESTIVALS AND LOCAL EVENTS

February/March
Granville: *Procession* on Carnival Sunday

March
Mortagne-au-Perche: *Foire au Boudin*, black pudding festival, third weekend in March

April
Rouen: *International 24-hour Boat Race* on the Seine from 30 April to 1 May

MARCO POLO SELECTION: FESTIVALS

1 **Bastille Day**
Major celebrations every year in most towns and villages (page 27)

2 **Balloon Festival**
Every two years hot-air balloon fans from all over the world come to Balleroy (page 28)

3 **Horse Parade**
See the horses in a unique setting at Haras-du-Pin (page 28)

4 **Torchlight procession**
Sailors' mass and torchlight parade in Granville (page 28)

5 **Polo and Grand Prix**
Elegant society event in the chic surroundings of Deauville (page 28)

6 **St Nicholas Market**
The Foire Saint-Nicolas in Evreux is popular with young and old (page 29)

May

Coutances: *Festival Jazz sous les Pommiers*
Cherbourg: *International Sailing Regatta*
Etretat: *Festival of the Sea*
Aigle: *The Four Days of Aigle*, after Ascension Day
Rouen: *Festival Jeanne d'Arc*
Honfleur: *Sailors' Pilgrimage* (Blessing of the Sea) Whitsun
Bernay: *Procession to Notre-Dame-de-la-Couture* on Whit Monday
Beuvron-en-Auge: *Foire aux Géraniums*, Geranium Festival

June

Le Havre: *International Sailing Regatta*
Deauville: *Horse racing*
★ Balleroy: if the year ends in an odd number the *International Balloon Festival* takes place on the second weekend in June

July

Carrouges: *Concerts in the courtyard*
Deauville: *Festivals, horse racing*
Bayeux: *Mediaeval Festival*
Domfront: *Folklore Festival*
Fécamp: *Festival of the Sea*, first weekend in July
Le Havre: *International Sailing Regatta*
Honfleur: *Festival of classical music*
La-Haye-de-Routot: *Saint Clair Firework Display* on 16 July
★ Granville: *Mass for sailors, with torchlight procession*, last Sunday
Camembert: *Fête de Camembert*, last Sunday

August

Livarot: *Fête du Livarot*, first weekend in August
Valognes: *The Valogne Concerts*, week-long music festival
Barneville-Carteret: *Festival of the Sea* in the middle of the month
Sainte-Marguerite: *Fishing Competition*, second Sunday
★ Deauville: *Polo Championship and Horse Sale* at the end of the month

September

Les Andelys: *Foire à tout*, general fair in the middle of the month
★ Haras-du-Pin: *Horse racing, demonstrations and horse-drawn carriage parade*, first Sunday

Lessay: *Foire Saint-Croix,* fair, 8–10 September
Deauville: *Festival du Cinéma Americain,* film festival
Avranches: *Fête des Trois Quartiers,* fair, third weekend in September
Alençon: *Cattle Market,* end of the month
Mont Saint Michel: *Autumn pilgrimage to celebrate the Archangel Michael,* at the end of the month
Lisieux: *Grandes Fêtes Thérésiennes,* Feast of Saint Theresa, *Open day at all historic monuments and museums,* penultimate weekend in September

October
Caen: *Tripes à la mode de Caen competition*
Pont d'Ouilly: *Foire de la Pomme,* Apple Fair
Haras-du-Pin: *horse racing and* a *horse-drawn carriage parade,* second Sunday
Vimoutiers: *Apple Fair with processions,* third weekend in October
Vire: *Foie-Gras Festival* at the end of the month

November
Vire: *Saveloy sausage market,* first weekend in November
Dieppe: *Foire aux Harengs,* third weekend in November
Beuvron-en-Auge: *Cider Festival*
St.-Valery-en-Caux: *Herring Fair*
Deauville: *Horse Sale*
Alençon: *National Steeplechase,* last Sunday in November

December
★ Evreux: *Foire Saint-Nicolas,* St Nicholas Fair on 6 December

A feast for the eyes for horse lovers: a carriage and four

GB
L341 YAY

The Seine Valley and the Alabaster Coast

Follow the loops of the Seine along the Abbey Trail and explore the steep cliffs of the wonderful Côte d'Albâtre

The very gentle incline of the Seine Valley means that the river wends its way round countless bends, some wide, others quite sharp, as it meanders down to the sea, gradually widening as it goes. The distance from Vernon to Le Havre is 300 km by boat. However, this is not the way to travel, if this is your first trip to Normandy. It's much better to take the metalled roads and cobbled lanes instead. For the jewels of this historically and scenically impressive Département are strung one after the other like pearls on a necklace. Rouen alone boasts a whole range of attractions and the towns and villages on either side of the regional capital are no less impressive. One thing to remember is that there are very few bridges over the wide river, so it is important to plan your journey carefully. At the end of the *Cap de la Hève* the unending battle of the steep coastline begins. It is a battle fought ceaselessly between

The Gros-Horloge in the street of the same name in Rouen: over the centuries the clock has continued to keep perfect time

Hotel and restaurant prices

Hotels
Category L: from 1,000 FF
Category 1: 500–1,000 FF
Category 2: 300–500 FF
Category 3: up to 300 FF

Based on the price per night of a double room for two people.

Restaurants
Category L: from 500 FF
Category 1: 300–500 FF
Category 2: 150–300 FF
Category 3: up to 150 FF

Prices are for a three-course meal excluding drinks.

Important abbreviations

FF French franc
av. Avenue
bd. Boulevard
pl. Place

the soft chalk cliffs and the constantly gnawing waves. Rivers have carved clefts in the 200-metre-high plateau, creating interesting harbours and wonderful bathing beaches. Your worst fears may well be confirmed here, as the tourist invasion in the *Val de Seine* and on the *Côte d'Albâtre* is immense, especially during the holiday season. Inland it is a very different story. The wide open space of the tranquil *Pays de Bray* is used for agriculture and boasts its own attractions. For instance, cider from *Longueville* and Neufchâtel cheese from *Neufchâtel-en-Bray*. On balance, the *Seine-Maritime* Département has something to offer all its visitors, whatever their tastes.

DIEPPE

(104/C2) Situated on the Arques estuary, Dieppe nestles between steep chalk cliffs. The town has a population of 40,000 and much of it still retains a mediaeval air. Its ideal location meant Dieppe was predestined to be an important harbour which offered safe anchorage to ships over many centuries, although it was often embroiled in fighting. The most recent example of this was in 1942 at the time of the Allies' failed invasion. Today large passenger steamers and ferries put in here. Dieppe is also an important trading centre. One of the goods to be imported was ivory and the art of ivory carving thrived and remains inextricably linked with the city.

The continuing popularity of France's oldest seaside resort for holiday-makers is due chiefly to the beautiful sandy beach just outside the town which is 2 km long at low tide. There are hotels in every price category along the promenade.

SIGHTS

Castle

On a cliff on the west side of the town is the massive fortress (15th century) which was built as a defence against the English. The oldest part of the building is the round tower (14th century) around which the rest of the castle developed. The square tower was not erected until the 17th century. The castle museum houses an interesting collection which includes 16th century ivory carvings.

Le Pollet

The old fishing quarter on the right-hand side of the Arques, with its winding lanes and narrow flights of steps is a great place for a romantic stroll. There are two lovely wall paintings in the church of *Notre-Dame-de-Grèves.*

Les Tourelles

Once there were six gates to the town (14th century) but only the "Harbour Gate", used as a prison during the French Revolution, still survives.

Place du Puits Salé

★ This little square with its fountain is right at the centre of the town. It is dominated by the lovely Norman gabled house – the *Café des Tribunaux* (17th century). Nearby is the church of *Saint-Rémy* (16th/17th century), with some remarkable wood panelling inside.

Saint-Jacques

It is not far along the *rue St-Jacques* to the splendid Gothic church of *Saint-Jacques* (13th to 16th century) with its 41-metre-high square tower and beautiful rose window above the west portal. Note also the interesting Chapel of the Holy Sepulchre (15th century).

MUSEUM

Musée du Château

In the castle high above the town is the interesting municipal museum which houses a valuable collection of ivory carvings. In addition, visitors can also admire paintings by Auguste Renoir, Raoul Dufy and Georges Braque. *Rue Chastes; daily except Tues 10 am–12 pm and 2 pm–5 pm; Sun 2 pm–6 pm; admission 13 FF*

RESTAURANTS

La Marmite Dieppoise

Serves excellent fish and shellfish dishes. *8, rue Saint-Jean; Tel. 02 35 84 24 26; category 2*

La Mélie

Likewise recommended for seafood lovers. *2, Grande Rue du Pollet; Tel. 02 35 84 21 19; category 2*

Le Panoramic

On the top floor of the *Hotels La Présidence* with a view of the coastline. Good Norman cuisine. *1, bd. de Verdun; Tel. 02 35 84 31 31; category 2*

MARCO POLO SELECTION: SEINE-MARITIME

1 **Rouen**
Brimming with jewels from the most magnificent treasure chest in Normandy (pages 40, 41)

2 **Fécamp**
Seaside resort with wonderful beige and gold cliffs along its chalk coastline (page 38)

3 **Etretat**
The fascinating "Needle" and the limestone archway which projects into the sea (page 37)

4 **Jumièges**
The abbey church of Notre-Dame, the most impressive ruin in Normandy (page 42)

5 **Destinations along the Abbey Trail**
Château d'Orcher and Saint-Martin-de-Boscherville contain fine examples of religious art (pages 38, 43)

6 **Dieppe**
The Place du Puits Salé with the gabled house – the Café des Tribunaux (page 32)

7 **Le Tréport**
Beach holiday below the steep cliffs of the Côte d'Albâtre (page 34)

8 **Varengeville-sur-Mer**
The artists' village beloved of Georges Braque perches on the high cliff top (page 35)

SHOPPING

Naturally one of the main attractions of shopping in Dieppe is seafood. Visitors who come here in late autumn should try to get to the *Foire aux Harengs*, the Herring Fair, which takes place the third weekend in November. The colourful weekly market every Saturday is worth a visit.

HOTELS

Aguado
Comfortable three-star hotel right by the beach. Well-appointed rooms. *30, bd. de Verdun; 56 rms; Tel. 02 35 84 27 00; Fax 02 35 06 17 61; category 1*

La Présidence
Modern, well-run establishment also very close to the beach. Thalassotherapy. *1, bd. de Verdun; 89 rooms; Tel. 023 35 84 31 31; Fax 02 35 84 86 70; category 1*

SPORTS & LEISURE

In July the horse show on the beach is a popular attraction, as is the horse racing in August/September.

INFORMATION

Office de Tourisme
Pont Jehan Ango, quai du Carénage; Tel. 02 35 84 11 77; Fax 02 35 06 27 66

SURROUNDING AREA

Eu (105/D1)
The easternmost town on the Norman coast has a population of 5,000 and is also the oldest in the region (1151). At the viewpoint on the plateau above the town visitors can also see the former collegiate church of *Notre-Dame-et-Saint-Laurent* (12th century), an impressive example of Norman Early Gothic architecture. The town's central focus is the Renaissance château (16th century) which is surrounded by a traditional French garden. The *Château d'Eu* was the favourite residence of King Louis-Philippe and he twice entertained the British Queen Victoria here. The chapel of the former Jesuit College, built in the style of Louis XIII, is also worth a visit. 36 km. Hotel: *Le Pavillon de Joinville*. Sophisticated château hotel. *Route du Tréport; 24 rooms; Tel. 02 35 50 52 52; Fax 02 35 50 27 37; category 1*

Le Tréport (105/D1)
★ The popular harbour town of Le Tréport (pop. 6,600) is romantically situated at the foot of the high cliffs in lovely surroundings. Together with the nearby seaside resort of *Mers-les-Bains* it has plenty to offer for holiday-makers and boasts a healthy climate rich in iodine. There are facilities for deep sea fishing and yachting and there is the sea and an indoor pool for bathing. The church of *Saint-Jacques* (16th century) is built on a hill high above the town. It has an impressive Renaissance portal and is well worth a visit. 32 km. A few kilometres away 378 steps take you up to the viewpoint known as *Calvaire des Terrasses* which affords a lovely panoramic view. Hotel/restaurant: *La Vieille Ferme*, old farmhouse with a rustic atmosphere. *Mesnil-Val; 23, rue de la Mer; 34 rooms; Tel. 02 35 86 72 18; Fax 02 35 86 12 67; category 2*

Miromesnil **(104/C2)**
Surrounded by a picturesque park and garden near Aubin-sur-Scie is the *Château de Miromesnil* (16th/17th century). The elegant façade is most impressive. It is said that Guy de Maupassant was born here. *1 May–15 Oct daily except Tues 9 am–12 am and 2 pm–6 pm; admission 30 FF.* 6 km

Varengeville-sur-Mer **(104/C2)**
★ The "artists' village" is situated high on the cliffs, surrounded by hedges. Built in the style of an Italian villa, the *Manoir d'Ango* (16th century; *daily 10 am–12.30 pm and 2.30 pm – 6.30 pm; admission 25 FF)* is well worth a visit, as is the church with its stained glass window by Georges Braque.

The painter is buried in the churchyard here. There is also a wonderful view of the cliffs and coastline. The brilliant floral splendour of the Parc Floral du Bois des Moutiers will thrill flower-lovers. 8km

Church window designed by Georges Braque, Varengeville-sur-Mer

LE HAVRE

City Map inside back cover

(103/D-E3) On the north side of the 9-km-wide Seine estuary lies the large industrial port of Le Havre (pop. 250,000). It was founded in the 16th century, when the older harbour of nearby Harfleur became silted up. It rapidly developed to become an important centre for shipping and is quite rightly also known as *La Porte Océane*, the Gateway to the ocean. Today Le Havre is the second largest sea port in France and lies at an important intersection of European transport routes. In 1945 the town was destroyed almost completely and had to be reconstructed from scratch. It is now a sprawling modern city with a dismally repetitive and linear architectural style which makes for a wearisome trek between the few sights it can muster. Le Havre has the most to offer to water sports enthusiasts. With its famous yachting marina, the city is a major centre for sailing aficionados and the beach at *Sainte-Adresse* is very popular.

SIGHTS

Espace Oscar Niemeyer
Approaching the centre of the city along a broad avenue, you can hardly miss the *Espace Oscar Niemeyer*, the immense cultural centre which was named after the Brazilian architect who designed

it. With a theatre, a cinema and extensive exhibition space, it forms the city's cultural focal point. Immediately opposite is its commercial counterpart: the *Bassin de Commerce* with the international trade centre.

Hôtel de Ville

Beyond the *Espace Oscar Niemeyer* is the *Place de l'Hôtel de Ville*, an enormous square in front of the town hall with its 72-metre-high tower. Along the edge of the square is the *Jardin Public* with a monument to commemorate the Résistance.

Notre-Dame

The main attraction at the port is the restored cathedral of *Notre Dame* (16th/17th century). It combines elements of both the Gothic and Renaissance styles. The square bell tower is very prominent. Inside, note the organ which was presented by Cardinal Richelieu in 1638.

Port de Plaisance

One attraction is without doubt the yachting marina, *Port de Plaisance* with room for over 1,000 boats. From the *Mole Digue Nord*, the panoramic view soon has visitors reaching for their cameras.

Sainte-Adresse

This once thriving harbour town has now become a north-western suburb of Le Havre and is a popular bathing resort. It is also worth visiting for the beautiful panoramic view from near the neo-Gothic chapel dedicated to *Notre-Dame-des-Flots.* Nearby are the rock formations of the *Cap de la Hève* and the old *Fort de Sainte-Adresse.*

Saint-Joseph

The modern steel and concrete construction of the church of *Saint-Joseph*, designed by city planner Auguste Perret, has a 106-metre-high, octagonal central tower. The square structure is interspersed with colourful little traceried lights.

MUSEUMS

Musée de l'Ancien Havre

The museum is in one of the oldest houses in Le Havre. Dozens of old plans, documents and pictures vividly illustrate the history of the city and the port. *1, rue Jérôme-Bellarmato; Wed–Sun 10 am–12 am and 2 pm–6 pm; admission 10 FF*

Musée des Beaux-Arts André Malraux

The Museum of Fine Arts is housed in a well-designed steel and glass building by the harbour. It is one of the best galleries in France, especially for modern art, and also boasts works by the major Impressionists. *Daily except Mon 11 am–6 pm, Sat and Sun until 7 pm; admission 25 FF. Bd. J. F. Kennedy*

Musée du Prieuré de Graville

The sculpture museum in the Graville priory church of *Sainte-Honorine* (11th century), with its splendid capitals, is well worth a visit. *Rue Elysée-Reclus; Wed–Sun 10 am–12 am and 2 pm–6 pm; admission 10 FF*

RESTAURANT

Petite Auberge

Good cuisine at reasonable prices. *32, rue Ste-Adresse; Tel. 02 35 46 27 32; category 2*

HOTELS

Clarine
Centrally-located hotel *Quai Colbert; 86 rooms; Tel. 02 35 26 49 49; Fax 02 35 25 10 13; category 2*

Ibis Le Havre Center
Peaceful hotel in the centre of the city. Friendly atmosphere. *Rue du 129ème Régiment d'Infanterie; 86 rooms; Tel. 02 35 22 29 29; Fax 02 35 21 00 00; category 2*

SPORTS & LEISURE

The *Port de Plaisance* bustles with activity during the holiday season. The high point is the international regatta in June.

INFORMATION

Office de Tourisme
Place de l'Hôtel de Ville; Tel. 02 32 74 04 04; Fax 02 35 42 38 39

SURROUNDING AREA

Cany Barville (103/F2, 104/B2)
This lively little town nestles in the picturesque valley of the River Durdent. The town hall is a remarkable building with four wings around a large forecourt.

However, the real attraction is to be found 2 km to the south on the left bank of the river. Situated in the middle of a park modelled on the English design is the *Château de Cany* (17th century). The stately château reflects the splendour of the age of Louis XIII both inside and out. *July–Aug daily except Fri 10 am–12 am and 3 pm–6 pm; admission 26 FF.* 56 km

Etretat (103/E2)
★ Once a quiet fishing village, Etretat has become a charming and lively bathing resort (pop. 1,600) which attracts many visitors all year round. This is due largely to the imposing natural backdrop of limestone to the left and right of the pebbly beach. To the west is the *Falaise d'Aval* with a view of the amazing Aiguille ("Needle") and the impressive arch which projects into the sea. On the eastern side is the *Falaise d'Amont* which affords a wonderful panoramic view of the town and its photogenic rock formations. In the town itself visitors

All kinds of animals

The region was covered with wonderful mixed forest, making it a paradise for animals. Over the course of time the woods were cleared and transformed into profitable arable land and the wild animals which had thrived there lost their natural habitat. Nevertheless there are still plenty of deer, as well as rabbits and hares. This is much to the delight of the farmers who have a great passion for hunting and go out into the fields with their shotguns after the harvest. Meanwhile, in the sometimes calm, sometimes turbulent waters of the lakes and ponds, trout, whitefish, pike, dace, eels and perch still survive unscathed. Thus, it is hardly surprising that there are large numbers of keen anglers. Visitors who share this particular passion will certainly enjoy accompanying them.

can see the *Château des Aigues,* the church of *Notre-Dame* and the Old Town with its interesting market halls. 29 km

Restaurant: *Le Bicorne; 5, bd. René Coty; Tel. 02 35 29 62 22; category 2.* Hotel: *Le Donjon;* manor house on the clifftop with a view of the coastline. *Chemin de Saint-Clair; 8 rooms; Tel. 02 35 27 08 23; Fax 02 35 29 92 24; category 1.* For those who like bizarre rock formations: continue 4 km to the *Cap Antifer,* where there is another "Needle" called the *Aiguille Belval.*

Fécamp (103/E2, 104/A2)

★ Framed by beach and cliff, the old seaside resort of Fécamp (pop. 25,000) is picturesquely situated at the bottom of a valley in the *Pays de Caux.* Its popularity as a bathing resort has survived the years, as has its importance as a cod fishing harbour. The former abbey church of *Sainte-Trinité* (12th century) and the massive Early Gothic structure which superseded it attracted many pilgrims in the past. Opposite the church, the ruins of a palace (10th/11th century) date from when the town was still the residence of the Dukes of Normandy. The Old Town is also interesting and, on the way to the harbour, there is the *Musée de la Bénédictine,* in which the well-known liqueur, made from the herbs of this rocky region, was distilled. Be sure to visit and sample the famous beverage. *110, rue Alexandre-le-Grand; daily 9.30 am–6 pm; admission 27 FF.* 40 km.

Restaurants: *l'Escalier, 101, quai Bérigny; Tel. 02 35 28 26 79; category 2. Le Vicomté; 4, rue Président Coty; Tel. 02 35 28 47 63; category 3.* Hotels: *d'Angleterre.* Hotel with a good restaurant; *93, rue de la Plage; 32 rooms; Tel. 02 35 28 01 60; Fax 02 35 28 62 95; category 3.* The *Ferme de la Capelle* is a pleasant, popular hotel. *Côte de la Vierge; 17 rooms; Tel. 02 35 29 12 19; Fax 02 35 28 70 55; category 2*

Harfleur (103/E3)

This suburb (pop. 9,700) on the eastern edge of the city is popular with visitors because of its lively Sunday market. In the centre of Harfleur is the famous *Église Saint-Martin,* a Gothic priory church with five aisles (14th – 16th century). As the harbour silted up, it gradually fell into decline. 5 km

★ Only 2 km away, situated on a hill above the Seine and surrounded by a lovely park, is the *Château d'Orcher* (18th century). The massive fortified tower, lined with battlements, dominates the whole castle complex. *Daily except Thurs 8 am–8 pm; castle 2 pm – 6 pm; admission 20 FF*

Veulettes-sur-Mer (103/F1)

This enchanting bathing resort, situated in the *Pays de Caux* on the Durdent estuary, boasts a splendid 1.5-km-long beach promenade. 66 km

Further along the coast towards Dieppe are a number of lovely little bathing resorts which nestle on the river estuaries. With their fine sandy beaches, Petites Dalles, Grandes Dalles, Saint-Valery-en-Caux, Veules-les-Roses, Sotteville, Saint-Aubin-sur-Mer, Quiberville, Sainte-Marguerite and Pourville, offer all the seaside fun the beach lover could wish for.

Yvetot **(103/F2, 104/B3)**
The major destruction wrought by World War II means that only a few traces remain of the glittering capital (pop. 11,000) of the former kingdom of the *Pays de Caux*. Thus the pride of the town today is the modern church of *Saint-Pierre* which was built in 1956. The *Musée du Pays de Caux*, an agricultural heritage museum, is worth a visit. *15 Mar–15 Nov daily except Tues 2 pm–6 pm; admission 25 FF.* 51 km. Hotel: *Hôtel du Havre; place Belge; 28 rooms; Tel. 02 35 95 16 77; Fax 02 35 95 21 18; category 2/3*

ROUEN

City Map inside back cover

(104/B-C4) The importance of this famous city on the Seine is undisputed. With a population of 120,000, it is the capital of the region and also of the Département. Situated 90 km inland from the coast, no one would guess that Rouen is the fifth largest seaport in France and that more agricultural products are exported from here than from any other French port. Every year, over 3,500 ships sail up the river to Rouen and then back down to the sea, demonstrating how the city's economic importance is inextricably linked with the Seine and the sea. Over the course of Rouen's eventful two-thousand-year history, the city's ideal location on a sharp bend in the river exercised an almost magical attraction for historic events. The most famous and tragic of these was when Joan of Arc was burnt at the stake in the *Place du Vieux-Marché.* The royal seat of the Dukes of Normandy suffered many trials and setbacks but also experienced a great many triumphs and prosperous periods. Thus, not only did a strong commercial base develop, but the city also boasts a sumptuous mediaeval centre. The rich architectural heritage found in the wonderful churches, splendid châteaux and impressive dwelling houses in a range of different styles have earned Rouen the nickname of "Museum City" and it is easy to see why. A stroll through the narrow streets and alleyways of this ancient city is without doubt an unforgettable experience.

Le Pont de Normandie: the longest cable-stayed bridge in the world

SIGHTS

Abbaye Saint-Ouen

The narrow *rue Damiette* leads to the church which belonged to a Benedictine abbey (14th – 16th century) founded in the Carolingian period. It is a splendid Gothic building with a magnificent crossing tower. Inside, note the beautiful 15th-century window and fine 16th-century organ. On the north side is the ruined cloister. *Daily Mar–Oct 10 am–12 pm and 2 pm–6 pm; Nov–Feb Wed, Sat and Sun only*

Aître de Saint-Maclou

★ Behind the church, in the *rue Martainville,* hidden along an inconspicuous passageway and surrounded by half-timbered houses, is the former charnel house (16th century). Here, stacked in wooden galleries decorated with intricate carvings, are many of the city's plague victims. *186, rue Martinville; daily 8 am–8 pm*

Beffroi and Gros-Horloge

★ Built into the Renaissance archways of the lively *rue du Gros-Horloge* is the *Gros Horloge* (Big Clock, 16th century). The clock has elaborate faces on both sides and remains an accurate timepiece to this day. ☀ The *Beffroi* (14th century) is the oldest part of the structure and affords a wonderful panoramic view over the historic city centre with its many lovely half-timbered houses. *Book at the Musée des Beaux Arts*

Hôtel de Bourgthéroulde

In the *place de la Pucelle* is this magnificent Gothic palace (16th century) with a Renaissance colonnade and some lovely reliefs.

Notre-Dame

★ The centrepiece of the Old Town, and undoubtedly one of France's most beautiful religious buildings, is the Gothic cathedral (12th–16th century). The

A dignified seat of jurisdiction: the Palais de Justice in Rouen

west front is particularly magnificent. It is flanked on the left-hand side by the *Tour de Saint-Roman* and on the right-hand side by the later *Tour de Beurre* (16th century). This tower's curious name means "Butter Tower" and derives from the fact that it was financed through the "Butter Pence" paid by the wealthy. At 152 m, the equally impressive crossing tower is the tallest church tower in France. Of particular interest inside are the crypt, the Lady Chapel and the tombstones of the Cardinals of Amboise. During the summer and at weekends the cathedral is atmospherically floodlit. *Daily 8 am– 7 pm; Sun 8 am–6 pm*

Palais de Justice

In the *Rue aux Juifs* is the splendid Palace of Justice in which the Normandy parliament used to sit. The building (16th century) is a fine example of the Flamboyant Gothic and Renaissance styles. During restoration work, remains of a synagogue (12th century) were found in the *Cour d'Honneur. Guided tours in the summer Sun 11 am, otherwise Sat 2 pm*

Place du Vieux-Marché

★ The old market square, which is lined with Norman half-timbered buildings and the modern church of *Sainte-Jeanne-d'Arc*, was the site where, on 30 May 1431, the Maid of Orleans was burnt at the stake. There is a monument commemorating her and opposite the church is the *Musée Jeanne d'Arc. Daily 9.30 am–6.30 pm; in winter 10 am–12 am and 2 pm–6 pm; admission 22 FF*

Saint-Maclou

From the cathedral, the *rue St-Romain*, with its exquisite half-timbered buildings, leads to the *Place Barthélémy* which boasts a real jewel of the Late Gothic style: the church of *Saint-Maclou* (15th–16th century). It has a splendid porch with five round arches and lots of filigree ornamentation. *Daily 10 am–12 am and 2 pm–6 pm*

MUSEUMS

Musée des Beaux-Arts

The Museum of Fine Arts boasts a wonderful collection of sculptures and paintings. These include a series of Impressionist paintings by Claude Monet, Auguste Renoir and Alfred Sisley. *Square Verdrel; daily except Tues 10 am–12 am and 2 pm–6 pm; admission 20 FF*

Musée le Secq-des-Tournelles

The former church of Saint-Laurent now houses a fantastic exhibition of wrought ironwork comprising more than 14,000 different items. *Rue Jacques-Villon; daily except Tues 10 am – 12 am and 2 pm –6 pm; admission 13 FF*

RESTAURANTS

Au Bois Chenu

An extremely pleasant restaurant which serves traditional cuisine. *Place Pucelle d'Orleans; Tel. 02 35 71 19 54; category 2*

Gill

An excellent place to sample Norman specialities. *9 quai de la Bourse; Tel. 02 35 71 16 14; category 1*

La Couronne

The oldest restaurant in France is housed in a splendid half-timbered building. The atmosphere and the food are of a high standard. *31, pl. du Vieux Marché; Tel. 02 35 71 40 90; category 1*

Les P'tits Parapluies

The restaurant is in a 16th-century house and furnished in the style of the turn of the last century. However, the sophisticated recipes are 21st-century. *Place Rougemare; Tel. 02 35 88 55 26; category 2*

SHOPPING

Rouen is famous for its beautiful faïences. There are many shops in which it is well worth having a browse.

HOTELS

Hôtel de Bordeaux

A friendly international hotel not far from the cathedral. *9, pl. de la République; 48 rooms; Tel. 02 35 71 93 58; Fax 02 35 71 92 15; category 2*

Hôtel de Dieppe

A hotel with a pleasant atmosphere close to the city centre. *Pl. Bernard-Tissot; 42 rooms; Tel. 02 35 71 96 00; Fax 02 35 89 65 21; category 1–2*

Mercure Rouen Centre

This modern hotel is situated right in the heart of the city. Lovely atmosphere. *Rue Croix-de-Fer; 125 rooms; Tel. 02 35 52 69 52; Fax 02 35 89 41 46; category 1*

INFORMATION

Office de Tourisme

25, pl. de la Cathédrale; Tel. 02 32 08 32 40; Fax 02 32 08 32 44

SURROUNDING AREA

Caudebec-en-Caux (103/F3)

For centuries the little village (pop. 2,700), situated on the right bank of the Seine and surrounded by woodland, depended on the Seine shipping for its livelihood. The *Musée de la Marine de Seine* vividly portrays the history of the village with diagrams and an excellent audio-visual display. This includes the fascinating natural spectacle of the *Mascaret*, the dangerous tidal wave which flooded the banks of the Seine at the turn of the tide until the riverbed was levelled. *Daily 2 pm–6.30 pm; admission 18 FF*

The magnificent, richly decorated 15th-century church of *Notre-Dame* is a masterpiece of the Flamboyant style. The 54-metre-high tower is one of the loveliest architectural monuments in Normandy. 35 km

Jumièges (104/B4)

★ The splendid Benedictine abbey complex (11th century) is undoubtedly one of the most impressive ruins in Normandy. Its earlier importance can still be felt today. The centrepiece is formed by the monastic church of *Notre-Dame* (11th century). Its two 43-metre-high towers give an idea of the building's original scale. One wall of the lantern tower (11th century) still stands. There are a few pre-Romanesque remnants of the *Église Saint-Pierre*. The surviving elements of the abbey buildings include a stone staircase, parts of the chapter house and the "Grand Cellier". *In summer daily 9 am–6.30 pm; admission 26 FF.* 27 km

The Abbaye de Jumièges was once rich and powerful and the abbey has lost nothing of this feeling despite it being a ruin

Martainville (104/C4)
Surrounded by a large wall and protected by a moat and four corner towers is the *Château de Martainville* (15th century), originally planned as a defensive structure. It now houses the *Musée départemental des Traditions et Arts Normands*, which illustrates the history of Norman furniture and domestic implements. *Daily except Tues 10 am–12.30 pm and 2 pm – 6 pm; admission 20 FF.* 16 km

Saint-Martin-de-Boscherville (104/B4)
★ This little town lies in a peaceful wooded landscape. It is best known for the great abbey church of *Saint-Georges* (12th century) which is built in the Norman Romanesque style. The appeal of the well-balanced building lies in the simple portal and the eight-bay nave. The harmonious round arch façade of the chapter house with its ambulatory is particularly fine. *Daily 9 am–12 am and 2 pm–5 pm; in summer 9 am–7 pm; admission 25 FF.* 8 km

Saint-Maurice-d'Ételan (103/F3)
The fine *Château d'Ételan* (15th century) enjoys a picturesque location in the middle of an old park. The château owes its charm not least to its Flamboyant Gothic architecture. *15 July – 30 Aug daily except Tues 2.30 pm–6.30 pm; admission 20 FF.* 46 km

Saint-Wandrille-Rançon (103/F3)
The monks of this Benedictine abbey (7th century) which lies in the Seine Valley knew little peace. Time and time again they were driven out, yet they always returned. The original buildings no longer exist. In the park is the interesting little chapel of *Saint-Saturnin* (10th century) and the ruins of the abbey church (13th–14th century).

In the present church, which was originally built as a tithe barn and was brought here from la Neuville de Bosc, the wooden construction and cloister (14th–15th century) can be seen. The abbey buildings (14th–15th century) are now inhabited and maintained by monks of the *Congragation of Solesmes.* The mass here is accompanied by their Gregorian chants. *Guided tours daily 3 pm–4 pm; Sun also 11.30 pm; admission 10 FF.* 34 km

Either side of the Seine Valley

A swathe of countryside, divided by the Seine, links the peaceful inland region with the lively coastline

The route to the *Côte Fleurie*, the favourite summer destination of the Parisians, goes through the Département of Eure. The road wends its way through a landscape which is naturally shaped to a great extent by the Seine. Nevertheless, both the smaller eastern part and the extensive western part also have their own individual character. So visitors should not restrict themselves to Giverny, Vernon, Gaillon and Les Andelys in the *Val de Seine*, but should explore the abbeys in the woods around Lyons on the right-hand side of the river and the historic architectural monuments in the *Pays d'Ouche* on the left. Once they reach the *Côte du Grâce*, visitors will have come to know and love a whole cross-section of Normandy.

EVREUX

(104/C6, 109/D1) The pleasant Département capital (pop. 52,000) is situated in the wonderful landscape of the *Pays d'Ouche*. Unfortunately, fate has not always been kind to Evreux. Both at the time of the French Revolution and later, during World War II, the town suffered major destruction. However, Evreux has been successfully rebuilt and, through its role as Département centre, the town has managed to develop to become an important trading and industrial centre. Nowadays this town, with its numerous historic places of interest, is flourishing in the middle of a burgeoning commercial centre.

The cathedral of Notre-Dame, Evreux

SIGHTS

Couvent des Capucins

Near the pretty *Jardin public* is an attractive building of harmonious design. It is the former Capuchin convent, the *Couvent des Capucins* (17th century). Be sure not to miss the beautiful cloister.

Notre-Dame

★ The turbulent history of the town was always inextricably linked with the mighty cathedral of *Notre-Dame*. Time and time again the buildings on this site were destroyed. Between the 12th and 17th centuries, however, the cathedral gradually developed its current impressive form. Inside, there are wonderful stained-glass windows (16th century) and fine Renaissance woodwork in the choir chapels. *Daily 7 am–12 am and 2 pm–7 pm*

Palais Épiscopal
The former Bishop's Palace is connected to the cathedral by a cloister. The splendid building now houses a museum in which a range of archaeological finds are displayed.

Saint-Taurin
The *Promenade des Remparts* along the little River Iton leads to the former abbey church of *Saint-Taurin* (10th–15th century) which was erected above the tomb of the saint, the first Bishop of the Evreux. Inside, the famous reliquary shrine is an extraordinary masterpiece of French gold work which dates back to the 12th century. *Daily 8.30 am–7 pm*

Tour de l'Horloge
Past the art gallery and the municipal theatre, opposite the town hall is the slim, elegant tower of the *Beffroi* (15th century), the symbol of the town. In the 44-metre-high watch tower hangs a bell. It weighs 2 tonnes and in the past it was rung to warn the people of Evreux of approaching danger of all kinds.

MUSEUM

Musée Municipal
The principle focus of the museum in the Bishop's Palace is archaeology. One of the main exhibits is a 60-metre-long piece of the town walls. *Daily except Mon 10 am–12 am and 2 pm–6 pm; Sun 2 pm–6 pm; admission free*

RESTAURANTS

L'Auberge de Parville
A typical restaurant with a good atmosphere, *grand service. 4 km out of the town, Parville, RN 13; Tel. 02 32 39 36 63; category 2*

Le Français
Very pleasant atmosphere with excellent Norman cuisine. *Pl. Clémenceau; Tel. 02 32 33 53 60; category 2*

HOTELS

De France
A hotel rich in tradition in the town centre. *29, rue Saint-Thomas; 16 rooms; Tel. 02 32 39 09 25; Fax 02 32 38 38 56; category 2*

Normandy
Set in a pretty, Norman, half-timbered building. Pleasant atmosphere. *37, rue Édouard Feray; 25 rooms; Tel. 02 32 33 14 40; Fax 02 32 31 24 74; category 2*

INFORMATION

Office de Tourisme
3, pl. du Général de Gaulle; Tel. 02 32 24 04 43; Fax 02 32 31 28 45

SURROUNDING AREA

Anet (109/E2)
The village lies on the south-eastern edge of Normandy on the River Eure. The *Château d'Anet* (16th century) belonged to Diane de Poitiers, Duchess of Valentinois and favourite of King Henry II. The well-preserved remains reveal a splendidly appointed Re-

MARCO POLO SELECTION: EURE

1 Evreux
The unique cathedral of Notre-Dame (page 45)

2 Beaumesnil
Wonderful Baroque château with fine sculptures (page 47)

3 Bernay
The Abbaye Notre-Dame, the oldest religious building in Normandie (page 47)

4 Giverny
The beautiful garden of the great Impressionist painter, Claude Monet (page 49)

5 Les Andelys
The fantastic view from the ruins of the once-powerful stronghold in the loop of the Seine (page 49)

naissance château. Well worth a visit. *In summer daily except Tues 2.30 pm–6.30 pm; Sun also 9 am–12 am; at other times Sun and holidays 2 pm–5 pm; admission 20 FF.* 34 km

Restaurant: *Moulin Ivry, Ivry-la-Bataille.* Excellent cuisine. *Terrace on the banks of the Eure; Tel. 02 32 36 40 51; category 1–2*

Beaumesnil (104/A6, 108/C1)
★ Set in splendid gardens and surrounded by a moat, the elegant Baroque château (17th century) is certainly on a par with the châteaux of the Loire. Built in the style of Louis XIII, one of the attractions of Beaumesnil is the central section decorated with lovely sculptures. Inside there is a little book-binding museum. *In summer daily except Tues 10 am–12 am and 2 pm–6 pm; admission 35 FF.* 39 km

Beaumont-le-Roger (103/F5)
The impressive ruins of the *Prieuré de la Trinité* (13th century) stand above the picturesque Risle Valley. In the town centre, the Renaissance church of *Saint-Nicolas* (13th–18th century) has some particularly fine glass. 26 km

Bernay (103/F5, 104/A5-6)
★ In the centre of this historic town (pop. 10,600) is one of Normandy's oldest churches, the *Eglise Abbatiale* (11th century). The beauty of the façades and well-balanced arcades of this Romanesque abbey church are of particular note. *In summer daily except Tues 10 am–12 am and 2 pm–7 pm; in winter Sun 10 am–12 am and 2 pm–5.30 pm; admission 8 FF.* 44 km

Restaurant: *Le Moulin Fouret,* former watermill, refined, delicious cuisine. *St-Aubin-le-Vertueux; Tel. 02 32 43 19 95; category 1–2*

Brionne (103/F4, 104/B5)
During the turbulent Norman period, this old town in the verdant Risle Valley was extensively fortified (11th/12th century). All that remains is the *donjon,* from the foot of which there is a lovely panoramic view over the

Claude Monet's garden in Giverny with the lily pond

valley and woods. 40 km. Hotel: *Le Logis; 1, pl. Saint-Denis; 12 rooms; Tel. 02 32 44 81 73; Fax 02 32 45 10 92; category 2*

The *Abbaye Le Bec-Hellouin* (11th century) is well worth a detour. The site includes the remains of the main church, the *Saint Nicolas* tower (15th century), the chapter house and the cloister (17th century). 6 km. Hotel/Restaurant: *Auberge de l'Abbaye*. The half-timbering is traditionally Norman, as is the food. *10 rooms; Tel. 02 32 44 86 02; Fax 02 32 46 32 23; category 3*

Conches-en-Ouche **(104/B6)**
This charming little town (pop. 3,500) is perched on a hill up above the River Rouloir. The *donjon* visible from here is what remains of a once powerful fortress dating from the 11th or 12th century. Not far away is the church of *Sainte-Foy*, which boasts an unusually fine tower (18th century) and 21 marvellous stained glass windows (16th century). *Daily 8 am–6.30 pm.* 18 km

Gaillon **(104/C5)**
On a rocky ledge above the Seine are the ruins of the *Château de Gaillon*. Very little remains of the original fortress but the ruins of the Renaissance pavilion and the gallery can still be admired. *July–Aug daily except Tues 9 am–12 am and 2 pm–6 pm; admission free.* 31 km

Gisors **(105/E5)**
The strategic importance of this town (pop. 9,000) can be seen very clearly in the castle (11th century) which dates from the period of the Norman Dukes and is very well-preserved.

The viewpoint at the foot of the two *donjons* affords a lovely panoramic view of the town and surrounding countryside. The church of *Saint-Gervais-et-Saint-Protais* (13th – 16th century), with its three-aisled chancel and Renaissance portal, is also worth visiting. *Daily 8.30 am–6 pm.* 53 km

Giverny **(105/D6, 109/E1)**
★ In the village of Giverny, at the point where the little River Epte flows into the Seine, is one of Normandy's greatest attractions: the house of the famous Impressionist Claude Monet.

The beautiful garden here was designed by Monet himself. All around the little Japanese bridge and the lily pond there is an abundance of plants and flowers, magnificent beyond compare. Since 1966 the property has belonged to the Academy of Fine Arts. *Apr–Oct daily except Mon 10 am–6 pm; admission 35 FF.* 35 km

Harcourt **(104/B5)**
Situated in a beautiful park full of exotic tree species is the *Château d'Harcourt* (12th century). The mediaeval building is protected by a 15-metre-deep moat and a massive wall with fortified defence towers. The extensive state forest which surrounds the château is a paradise for walkers and nature lovers. *In summer daily 10 am–7 pm, otherwise daily except Tues 2 pm–6 pm; admission 25 FF.* 36 km

Les Andelys **(104/C5)**
★ Perched on a sheer limestone cliff above a picturesque loop in the Seine and the quiet town of Les Andelys (pop. 10,000) are the massive ruins of the once-proud citadel, the *Château Gaillard.* It was built by Richard the Lionheart in 1196 over a period of two years and was an important stronghold in the Norman lines of defence against France. After his victory, King Henry IV had the castle slighted. The remains, the *donjon* which is surrounded by a moat and fortified wall, is just as photogenic as the marvellous panoramic view. *15 Mar–15 Nov daily, except Tues/Wed mornings, 9 am–12 am and 2 pm–6 pm; admission 18 FF.*

In Les Andelys itself, be sure to visit the former collegiate church of *Notre Dame* (12th century) with its lovely Renaissance portal. 40 km

Lisors **(103/E5, 108/B1)**
Nestling in a glade in the wonderful beechwoods of *Lyons*, the fine Cistercian Abbey of *Mortemer*

Château Gaillard above Les Andelys, destroyed by Henry IV

(12th century) is a real jewel. Many parts of the abbey building and one of the cellars still survive. Visitors can wander round the small museum of monastic life and go on a tour of the surrounding park in a little train. *Abbey, Easter–Sept daily 2 pm–6 pm; at other times Sun 2 pm–6 pm. Park all year round 9 am–1 pm and 2 pm–6.30 pm; admission 35 FF.* 60 km

Louviers (104/C5)
Situated just above where the Eure flows into the Seine is the little town of Louviers (pop. 20,000), best known for its textile industry. The church of *Notre-Dame* (13th century) has become famous as a fine example of Flamboyant Gothic architecture. The sumptuously decorated portal and the wonderful stained glass windows are of particular note. The *Couvent des Pénitents* has a unique cloister which runs along the water. The town museum has an astonishingly extensive collection of lovely faïences from all regions and periods. *Daily except Tues 10 am–12 am and 2 pm–6 pm; admission 10 FF.* 22 km

Lyons-la-Forêt (105/D4)
This picturesque village (pop. 1,000) is characterised by half-timbered buildings. The central focus is the open market hall (15th century) which is used as a venue for craft and cultural events. In addition, the village is a popular departure point for walkers and cyclists. The surrounding countryside, with its lovely beech woods is a real paradise for those who enjoy the peace and tranquillity of an unspoilt natural environment. 60 km

Pont-Audemer (103/F4, 104/A4)
Inland from the *Côte Fleurie*, the small, dreamy town of Pont-Audemer (pop. 10,000) on the Risle owes its charms to the many picturesque little lanes of half-timbered houses (16th century). In the centre is the church of *Saint-Ouen* (11th century), magnificent in design but never completed, and the Romanesque church of

The lovely half-timbered buildings of Vernon are just one of the town's attractions

In the spirit of Marco Polo

Marco Polo was the first true world traveller. He travelled with peaceful intentions forging links between the East and the West. His aim was to discover the world, and explore different cultures and environments without changing or disrupting them. He is an excellent role model for the travellers of today and the future. Wherever we travel we should show respect for other peoples and the natural world.

WWF

Saint-Germain (11th century). The town is a popular starting point for excursions into the *Vernier* marshes and the woods of *Brotonne*. 20 km east of Rouen.

Vascœuil **(104/C4)**
The *Château de Vascœuil* (12th century) is imposingly situated in the middle of a 5-hectare park. It is now classified as an historic monument and has been turned into an art gallery. Works by contemporary artists are exhibited in the château and dovecote, while sculptures can be seen in the park. *Daily 2.30 pm–6.30 pm; in summer 11 am–7 pm; admission to château and park 40 FF.* 60 km

Verneuil-sur-Avre **(108/C2)**
The well-preserved heart of this historically important town (pop. 7,000) on the Avre captivates visitors with its half-timbered buildings (15th/16th century) and impressive town houses (17th/18th century). The Benedictine church of *Saint-Nicolas* (15th century) and the Romanesque church of *Notre-Dame* (12th century), with some lovely sculptures, are well worth seeing. The 60-m-high *Tour de la Madeleine* affords a panoramic view and the *Parc Faugère* is perfect for a stroll along the town walls. 39 km. Hotel/restaurants: *Du Saumon; 89, pl. de la Madeleine; 29 rooms; Tel. 02 32 32 02 36; Fax 02 32 37 55 80; category 2. Le Clos*, Château-Hotel; *98, rue de la Ferté-Vidame; 10 rooms; Tel. 02 32 32 21 81; Fax 02 32 32 21 36; category 1. Moulin de Balisne; Balisne; 10 rooms; Tel. 02 32 32 03 48; Fax 02 32 60 11 22; category 2*

Vernon **(105/D6, 109/E1)**
The central focus of this vibrant town (pop. 23,600), with its many half-timbered houses (15th century), is the splendid Gothic collegiate church dating from the 12th century. On the right bank of the river, by a romantic bridge, are the ruins of a mediaeval château (13th century). In a half-timbered building is the *Musée Alphonse-Georges Poulain* (folk art and history); *12, rue du Pont; daily except Mon 11 am–1 pm and 2 pm–6 pm; admission 15 FF.* On the edge of the town you can admire the magnificent Italian-style *Château de Bizy* (18th century). There are some fine statues in the park near the stables. Museum: *in summer daily except Mon 10 am–12 am and 2 pm–6 pm; otherwise weekends 2 pm–5 pm; admission 34 FF.* 28 km. Hotel/restaurant: *Normandy; 1, av. Mendès-France; 50 rooms; Tel. 02 32 51 97 97; Fax 02 32 21 01 66; category 2*

Jouets au ballon rouge souvenirs
JOUETS - SOUVENIRS
CN 332249

Wind, water, waves and beaches ...

Wide sandy beaches for fun at the seaside and, further inland, a fertile landscape for peaceful relaxation

Everyone who comes here for a seaside holiday is enchanted by the heavenly sandy beaches along the coast of the Département of Calvados. The *Côte Fleurie,* the "Floral Coast", between Honfleur and Cabourg, delights visitors both with its exclusive Deauville and with its more family-oriented resorts clustered along the *Corniche Normande.* Somewhat more modest but equally delightful for a seaside vacation are the holiday resorts on the *Côte de Nacre.* The flat sandy beaches here are also known as the *Plages du Débarquement,* recalling the fact that this is where the Allies landed on D-Day. Bunkers and military cemeteries bear witness to the dramatic events which marked 1944. Sadly, these events also left their mark on the inland area, as there was hardly a village or town which did not endure terrible suffering. However, since then the region has recovered very well and most of the houses and architectural monuments have been carefully restored. It is well worth visiting the historic towns such as Caen, Lisieux or Bayeux, to admire the rare beauty of their buildings. It is a great experience to drive through the region and discover the countless treasures it contains. The delights of the Calvados countryside are seasoned with unparalleled culinary delicacies. This naturally includes the "Three Cs" but also encompasses a whole range of delicious specialities which make the heart of the gourmet beat faster. The Département of Calvados has so much to offer visitors who enjoy exploring and finding out more about where they are.

Trading centre, harbour town with a seafaring past and an artists' colony: Honfleur has all the necessary ingredients for a real Norman holiday

BAYEUX

(101/F3, 102/B3) The old capital of Bayeux (pop. 16,000) is situated on the fertile plains of the mainly agricultural *Bessin.* Its original character as an historic centre has been very well preserved. This is not least due to the fact that, unlike most other towns in Normandy, Bayeux survived World War II intact. And so the splendid 11th-century Gothic cathedral of

Notre-Dame, which stands right in the centre of the pleasant Old Town, remains a great attraction. The little mediaeval lanes are a wonderfully inviting place for a stroll. They are lined with venerable old town houses, with their slate roofs and copper guttering. The old town's second great attraction is, of course, the famous, skilfully embroidered Bayeux tapestry, which tells the story of William the Conqueror's victory over England in 70 metres of superbly detailed tableaux. This unique work of art provides an impressive insight into life in the 11th century.

SIGHTS

Old Town

A walk around the Old Town allows you to soak up the atmosphere of the old half-timbered and stone houses. Normandy's oldest half-timbered building is on the corner of the *Rue de Cuisiniers* and the *Rue Saint-Martin*. Then there are the mediaeval town houses in the *Rue Franche* and the *Hôtel du Croissant* in the *Rue Saint-Jean*. From the Aure Bridge there is a lovely view of the photogenic old watermill, *Croquevieille*. Right next to it is the former fish market.

MARCO POLO SELECTION: CALVADOS

1 **Caen**
With its splendid churches, Caen is one of the most impressive towns in Normandy (page 57)

2 **Côte Fleurie**
The dream coast – the Norman *Côte d'Azur* with wonderful bathing beaches (pages 64–66)

3 **Deauville**
Elegant seaside resort with an international flair, popular with high society (page 64)

4 **Trouville**
This pleasant bathing resort also boasts the remains of an old fishing harbour (page 64)

5 **Honfleur**
The romantic town of the Impressionists, full of picturesque images (page 62)

6 **Bayeux**
The ancient town with the impressive cathedral and, of course, the unique tapestry (page 55)

7 **Balleroy**
The fine château is an architectural masterpiece in the style of Louis XIII (page 56)

8 **Vaches Noires**
The impressive formations of dark brown marlaceous rock (page 65)

9 **Cabourg**
Marcel Proust's seaside resort with the friendly charm of the *Belle Époque* (page 66)

10 **Pointe du Hoc**
The breath-taking headland at the end of a spectacular stretch of coastline (page 67)

Notre-Dame

★ This is one of France's particularly beautiful old Gothic cathedrals (11th century). Little remains of the original Romanesque church, except for the crypt and the central core of the towers. The alterations to the Gothic choir (13th century) were followed by others, rarely to the transept, side aisle capitals and finally the crossing tower which was topped by a Baroque dome (18th century). Note the ornamentation on the walls of the nave. *Rue Bienvenu; daily 8 am–12.30 pm and 2.30 pm–7 pm; in summer 8 am–7 pm*

Tapisserie de Bayeux

★ The famous work of art can be seen in the *Centre Guillaume le Conquérant* in the *Rue Nesmond*. The tapestry was originally commissioned to be hung on the wall of the cathedral but is now housed in this specially converted building. Very crowded during the holiday season. *Daily 9.30 am–12.30 pm and 2 pm–6 pm; in summer 9 am–7 pm; admission 37 FF (4 museums)*

MUSEUMS

Musée Baron Gérard

As well as paintings (16th–19th century), the museum in the former Bishop's Palace houses a collection of lovely cushion lace and fayences. *Centre Guillaume le Conquérant; daily 10 am–12.30 pm and 2 pm–6 pm; June–Sept 9 am–7 pm; admission 37 FF (4 museums)*

Musée Diocésain d'Art Religieux

Collections of religious art, documents and manuscripts and valuable gold work. *Hôtel du Doyen; 6, rue Lambert-Leforestier; 1 July–31 Aug daily 10 am–12.30 pm and 2 pm–6 pm; admission 37 FF (4 museums)*

Musée Mémorial de la Bataille de Normandie

Documents, diagrams and films about the Allied landings. *Bd. Fabian-Ware; daily 10 am–12.30 pm and 2 pm–6 pm; June to Aug 9.30 am–6.30 pm; admission 30 FF*

RESTAURANTS

Les Arcades

Delicious, reasonably-priced fish and meat dishes. *10, rue Laitière; Tel. 02 31 92 72 79; category 3*

Le Baromètre

Dining at the lovely *Château de Goville* is an experience indeed. *Le-Breuil-en-Bessin; Tel. 02 31 22 19 28; category 1–2*

SHOPPING

In the artists' workshops visitors are not simply able to admire wooden, ceramic and porcelain items, they can also watch the artists at work. *5–11, pl. aux Pommes*

HOTELS

Château de Goville

The Château Hotel has a really wonderful atmosphere. 11 km west of Bayeux. *Le Breuil-en-Bessin; 9 rooms; Tel. 02 31 22 19 28; Fax 02 31 22 68 74; category 1*

Hôtel d'Argouges

A peaceful oasis not far from the historic heart of the town. *21, rue de Saint-Patrice; 25 rooms; Tel. 02 31 92 88 86; Fax 02 31 92 69 16; category 2*

Apple blossom: apples are an essential ingredient of many Norman delicacies

Le Lion d'Or
Former staging post situated right in the centre of the town. *71, rue Saint-Jean; 27 rooms; Tel. 02 31 92 06 90; Fax 02 31 22 15 64; category 1*

ENTERTAINMENT

🕺 The discos, *La Queue du Chat* in Etreham and *Le Royal* in the Hôtel de Brunville provide popular entertainment for younger visitors.

INFORMATION

Office de Tourisme
Pont Saint-Jean; Tel. 02 31 51 28 28; Fax 02 31 51 28 29

SURROUNDING AREA

Balleroy (101/F4, 102/B4)
★ In the extensive forest of Cérisy is the *Château de Balleroy* (17th century), a splendid building erected during the early years of Classicism in the style of Louis XIII. The elegant French ornamental garden and the lovely park complement the architectural layout of the estate.

The rich interior is also well worth seeing. *May–Oct daily except Wed 9 am–12 am and 2 pm–6 pm; admission 30 FF.* In the stables in front of the château is the *Musée des Ballons,* charting the history and development of hot-air ballooning. *May–mid Oct daily except Wed 9 am–12 am and 2 pm – 6 pm; admission 23 FF, together with the château 37 FF.* 18 km

Colombières (101/F4, 102/B4)
The château (15th century) on the edge of the *Aure* marshes is situated within a mediaeval fortress surrounded by a moat. The main part of the fortress is square in shape and flanked by towers. *Daily 10 am–*

12 am and 2 pm – 5 pm; admission 22 FF. 25 km

Creully **(102/C3-4)**
The turbulent history of the *Château de Creully* (11th–16th century) is closely linked with the history of the mediaeval village of Creully. In 1944, the powerful building with its fortified walls was used by the British General Montgomery as his headquarters and by the BBC as a broadcasting studio. *July – Aug daily 10 am–12 am and 3 pm – 6 pm; admission 15 FF.* 12 km. Hotel/restaurant: *Château du Baffy; Colombiers/Seulles; 35 rooms; Tel. 02 31 08 04 57; Fax 02 31 08 08 29; category 1*

Saint-Gabriel-Brecy **(102/B4)**
The *Prieuré Saint-Gabriel* was founded in the 11th century but buildings were erected and extended over many centuries. The main buildings, the priory church and the prison tower (15th century) are well worth seeing.

The former priory is now used as an agricultural college. *Daily 2 pm–7 pm; admission July/Aug 15 FF, free at all other times.* 12 km

Tour-en-Bessin **(101/F3, 102/B3)**
This church, with its elegant crossing tower (13th century) and unusual choir (15th century), dominates the village of Tour-en-Bressin.

At the northern edge of the village there is a long avenue leading to the pretty little *Château de Vaulaville* (18th century). Inside, visitors can admire some splendid woodwork, lovely furniture and a collection of Bayeux porcelain. *Mar–Nov 2.30 pm–6.30 pm; admission 15 FF.* 6 km

CAEN

☛ **City Map inside back cover**

(102/C4) ★ The town which was once the capital of the Duchy of Normandy ruled by William the Conqueror is situated on a wide plain, just 14 km from the sea. Caen (pop. 120,000) is now both the administrative centre of the Département of Calvados and the undisputed centre of the commercial and cultural life of *Basse-Normandie.* The university, which was founded in 1432 and is steeped in tradition, is one of the largest in the country. During the invasion in 1944 the town was almost completely destroyed. It was reconstructed in harmony with the character of the beautiful Old Town and its wonderful architectural monuments which fortunately survived the destruction.

SIGHTS

Abbaye aux Dames
In the eastern half of the Old Town is the nunnery which forms the counterpart to the Abbaye des Hommes; the equally impressive Romanesque church of *La Trinité,* the *Église de l'Abbaye aux Dames* (11th century). Visitors can admire the crypt with its cross vaults and the cloister. There is also a little French garden. *Pl. de la Reine Mathilde; guided tours daily 2.30 pm and 4 pm; admission free*

Abbaye aux Hommes
The best place to start a tour of the town is in the *Place Louis-Guillouard* at the monumental *Abbaye aux Hommes.* The abbey church of *St-Etienne* was built in the Romanesque style by

William the Conqueror in the 11th century. Two hundred years later the choir and towers in the Early Gothic style were added. The church is a captivating, aesthetic masterpiece of ecclesiastical architecture. The abbey building, added to the church in the 18th century, has some impressive interior ornamentation. *Guided tours daily 9.30 am–4 pm; admission 10 FF*

Château

The lively *Rue Saint-Pierre,* which boasts two lovely old half-timbered buildings, eventually brings you to an imposing fortress (11th century) which perches on a low rocky outcrop. Visitors can walk along the well-fortified circular wall, punctuated by two gateways and numerous ramparts. The walls afford a wonderful view over the fantastic townscape of Caen which is characterised by its towers.

Hôtel d'Escoville

Opposite the church, in the *Place Saint-Pierre* is the impressive Renaissance edifice of the *Hôtel d'Escoville* (16th century). The attractive courtyard is decorated with sculptures.

Leroy Tower

In the *Place Courtonne,* the *Leroy* Tower formed an important part of the town's fortifications.

Saint-Pierre

The Gothic church of *Saint-Pierre* (13th/14th century) stands in front of the castle in the *Place Saint-Pierre.* It has an impressive façade with ornamentation in the Flamboyant style and a 78-m-high Norman belltower.

MUSEUMS

Mémorial Caen Normandie

The *Musée pour la Paix* was officially opened in 1988 by President Mitterand. The museum uses the most up-to-date technology to provide illustrations and analyses of the invasion in World War II. *Esplanade Eisenhower; daily 9 am–7 pm; admission 50 FF*

Musée des Beaux-Arts

In the castle grounds is the art museum, with collections of Italian and French paintings (17th/18th centuries). *Esplanade du Château; daily except Tues 10 am–6 pm; admission 20 FF*

Caen by night has a majestic air

Musée de Normandie

This museum is also in the castle grounds, in the former governor's house. It provides a vivid and comprehensive illustration of the history of Normandy. *Esplanade du Château; daily 9.30 am–12.30 pm and 2 pm–6 pm; admission 10 FF*

RESTAURANTS

Alcide

Restaurant serving typical local dishes. *1, pl. Courtonne; Tel. 02 31 44 18 06; category 3*

Chantegrill

Grill restaurant. *17, pl. de la République; Tel. 02 31 85 23 64; category 3*

La Bourride

Top class restaurant which serves particularly fine fish and meat dishes. *15, rue de Vaugueux; Tel. 02 31 93 50 76; category 1*

SHOPPING

Caen, too, has its weekly markets selling a wide range of goods. They are lively affairs, Fri in the *Place St-Sauveur* and Sun in the *Place Courtonne.*

HOTELS

Le Dauphin

A very good hotel right in the town centre which also includes a restaurant. *29, rue Gémale; 22 rooms; Tel. 02 31 86 22 26; Fax 02 31 86 35 14; category 1*

Moderne

Also in the town centre. Breakfast on the fifth floor with a panoramic view. *116, bd. du Maréchal-Leclerc; 40 rooms; Tel. 02 31 86 04 23; Fax 02 31 85 37 93; category 1–2*

INFORMATION

Office de Tourisme

Pl. St-Pierre; Tel. 02 31 27 14 14; Fax 02 31 27 14 13

SURROUNDING AREA

Beuvron-en-Auge (103/D4)

On the *Cidre* Route, in the heart of the *Pays d'Auge*, the village is preserved as an historic monument. The old market place is surrounded by lovely, typically Norman, half-timbered houses. The highlight is the *Manoir* on the southern edge of the village. 27 km

Crèvecœur-en-Auge (103/D5)

The former *Manoir* is made up of an interesting collection of half-timbered buildings (11th-16th century) and is protected by a moat. Nearby is the castle, with its *donjon*. The estate now belongs to the Schlumberger Foundation which is also the subject of a small museum. *Apr–Sept daily 1 pm–6 pm; at other times by appointment (Tel. 02 31 63 02 45); admission 27 FF.* 28 km

Falaise (102/C5)

The main attraction of Falaise (pop. 8,500), birthplace of William the Conqueror, is the mighty fortress, built on a rocky outcrop. The oldest part is the square *donjon* (11th century). The remains of the castle walls can be seen, including a number of towers and gateways. The best known is the *Porte des Cordeliers.* Beneath the gatehouse is the *Église Sainte-Trinité* (13th–16th century), the individual elements of which provide a vivid illustration of the transition from the Gothic to the Renaissance styles.

The building of *Saint-Gervais* (12th–15th century) spanned the Romanesque and Gothic periods. Falaise, with its lovely gatehouses and town walls, was almost completely destroyed during World War II but has been rebuilt. 34 km. Hotel: *Château du Tertre; Saint-Martin-de-Mieux; 9 rooms; Tel. 02 31 90 01 04;. Fax 02 31 90 33 16; category 1*

Fontaine-Ètoupefour (102/C4)
South-west of Caen, surrounded by a moat, is the château of *Fontaine-Ètoupefour.* A drawbridge takes visitors across the moat to the gatehouse, embellished with charming towers (15th century). Beyond it are the ruins of the former château (16th century). 6 km

Fontaine-Henry (102/C4)
The majestic château (15th century) is situated in an enchanting park in the lovely valley of the Mue. It was built on to an earlier 12th-century fortified site. The château has a fine exterior, and also boasts a lovely interior. *Open daily by appointment (Tel. 02 31 80 00 42); admission 30 FF.* 23 km

Lisieux (103/E4)
The impressive centrepiece of the *Pays d'Auge* is the diocesan town of Lisieux (pop. 25,000), which is famous as a popular place of pilgrimage. The figure of the local saint, Thérèse Martin, is inextricably linked with the town. The cathedral of *Saint-Pierre* dates from the 12th century and, with its pair of Romanesque-Gothic towers, it demonstrates how styles changed as it was being built. Near the cathedral is the former Bishop's Palace (17th century), with its splendidly extravagant courtyard. There are some interesting half-timbered buildings in the Old Town.

On a hill on the south-east side of the town is the *Basilica of Sainte-Thérèse,* the famous place of pilgrimage, which has a 90-m-high dome. *Daily 8 am–6.30 pm; admission free.* 49 km. Hotels/restaurants: *Hôtel de l'Europe; 34, rue de la Gare; 24 rooms; Tel. 02 31 31 01 43; Fax 02 31 31 27 27; category 3. La Coupe d'Or; 49, rue Pont-Mortain; 18 rooms; Tel. 02 31 31 16 84; Fax 02 31 31 35 60; category 3*

Livarot (103/D5)
The town in the heart of the *Pays d'Auge* is home to the strong, aromatic *Livarot* cheese and boasts numerous manor houses and half-timbered buildings, as well as the *Musée du Fromage de Livarot* in the *Manoir de l'Isle (daily 10 am–12 am and 2 pm–6 pm; admission 12 FF).* 45 km

Mézidon-Canon (103/D5)
This quiet little town lies on the edge of the *Pays d'Auge,* along the green Dives Valley. It owes its historical significance to the attractive *Château Canon* (18th century). Built in the Italian style, the château is surrounded by a lovely garden and shady avenues. *Easter–30 Sept daily except Tues 2 pm–7 pm; admission 25 FF.* Don't miss the beautifully restored *Breuil* church (12th century) in Mézidon. 24 km

Pontécoulant (101/F5, 102/B5)
This lovely classical château (16th/18th century) is wonderfully situated in the Durance valley and is one of the most noticeable edifices in the Suisse Normande. Surrounded by an

A hidden château which is worth a detour: Saint-Germain-de-Livet

English park, it creates an imposing impression. It houses an interesting collection of furniture which is displayed in the *Musée Départemental. 16 Apr–30 Sept daily except Tues 10 am–12 am and 2.30 pm–6 pm; 1 Nov–15 Apr except Mon and Tues 2.30 pm–4.30 pm; Oct closed; admission 10 FF.* 49 km

Saint-Germain-de-Livet (103/E5)
This enchanting Renaissance château lies 8 km south of Lisieux in the Touques valley. A Norman half-timbered extension was built on to the lovely 14th century main house in the 16th century. The façade of the gate house and its slender *tourelles* are decorated with a chequered design. The courtyard includes Italian-style arcades. Fresco remnants can be seen in the half-timbered part. *Daily except Tues 10 am–12 am and 2 pm–5 pm; in summer until 7 pm; admission 33 FF.* 52 km

Saint-Pierre-sur-Dives (103/D4)
In the centre of this lovely village stands the market hall (11th/12th century) which is made of real Norman wood. After it was destroyed in 1944, the building was lovingly and authentically rebuilt. Every Monday the market hall is host to a colourful and very popular market. The Benedictine abbey church (11th century) is one of the most beautiful Gothic buildings in Normandy. 30 km

Thury-Harcourt (102/C5)
The village of Thury-Harcourt (pop. 1,700) lies on the edge of the Suisse Normande. It is famous for the *Château d'Harcourt* (17th century) which was burnt down in 1944. The ruins can be seen on the bank of the Orne surrounded by an English park (18th century) full of flowers. *1 Mar–15 Nov daily 2 pm–7 pm.* 26 km

Vire (101/E5, 102/A5, 107/D1)
This village (pop. 16,000) which is so rich in history is situated in the *Bocage Virois.* It is famous for the delicious local speciality, a smoked sausage which is known as *Andouille de Vire.* Visitors can go round the remains of the old 13th-century keep, the *Porte Horloge,* the church of *Notre-Dame* and the fortified towers of *Saint-Sauveur* and *Raines.* On a rocky outcrop are the ruins of an old defensive fortress (12th century) with its square *donjon.* There is a fantastic, panoramic view over the Vire valley and its ravines from here. 55 km

Hotel: *Hotel de France; 20 rooms; 4, rue d'Aignaux; Tel. 02 31 68 00 35; Fax 02 31 68 22 65; category 2–3*

HONFLEUR

(103/E3) ★ Honfleur (pop. 8,600) is one of the most attractive harbour towns on the Norman coast. It is an enchanting place to visit, situated in an ideal location on the Seine estuary. In the past it was the starting point for many daring seafarers setting out on voyages of exploration across the world's oceans. In 1608 the legendary Samuel de Champlain left from here to establish a French colony on the other side of the Atlantic in Québec. When the harbour was extended in the 17th century, trade began to flourish bringing new prestige to the fishing port. In the middle of the 19th century the Impressionist, Eugène Boudin, set up his painting school *Saint-Siméon,* drawing increasing numbers of famous Impressionists and established an artists' colony in his birthplace.

SIGHTS

Old Town
In the romantic *Sainte-Catherine* district, charming half-timbered buildings line the cosy little alleyways and lanes. The atmosphere here is imbued with the invitation to explore the area and tourists are only too happy to do so. Look out for the well-preserved salt warehouses in the *Rue de la Ville.*

Lieutenance
At the end of the harbour is the ancient stone building called the *Lieutenance* (16th/17th century), together with the remains of the old fortifications. The Lieutenance was formerly the Governor's residence and now houses the harbour office. The lock here allows boats to leave the harbour at high tide.

Mont Joli
A twisting road to the west of the town leads to the chapel of *Notre-Dame-de-Grâce* (17th century), with its fine slate-roofed tower. From the square in front of the pilgrims' chapel visitors can enjoy a wonderful panoramic view of the Seine estuary and the Pont de Tancarville.

Sainte-Catherine

In the Old Town, in the *Place Sainte-Catherine*, stands the impressive wooden church of *Sainte-Catherine* (15th century). It consists of two parallel naves and has a splendid free-standing belfry which is clad with chestnut shingling. *Daily 10 am–12 am and 2 pm–5 pm; in summer until 6 pm*

Saint-Étienne

The town's oldest church (14th century), with its slate-roofed tower, can be seen from the *Quai Saint-Étienne.*

Vieux Bassin

The Old Harbour (17th century), with its colourful yachts and boats, forms a picturesque centrepiece. The *Quai Sainte-Catherine* is a poetic gallery of lovely, narrow, slate-hurg houses. In the past it was painters who were drawn here, but now it is photographers who come to capture the essence of its delightful atmosphere.

MUSEUMS

Musée de la Marine

The museum boasts a large collection of model ships, as well as documenting the history of the seafarers who sailed from Honfleur. *Église Saint-Étienne; in summer daily, at other times weekends only, 10.30 am–12 am and 2.30 pm–6 pm; admission 25 FF*

Musée Eugène Boudin

The museum, named after the town's most famous son, includes collections of traditional Norman dress. *Pl.Erik-Satie; 15 Mar–30 Sept daily except Tues 10 am–12 am and 2 pm–6 pm; otherwise 2.30 pm–5 pm; admission 18 FF*

RESTAURANTS

L'Absinthe

Right by the harbour, delicious fish and seafood dishes. *10, quai de la Quarantaine; Tel. 02 31 89 39 00; category 2*

Le Belvédère

Excellent restaurant in a good hotel. Authentic Norman cuisine. *36, rue Emile-Rénouf; Tel. 02 31 89 08 13; category 2*

SHOPPING

The little town is still closely associated with art and boasts one gallery after another.

HOTELS

Ferme Saint-Siméon

Once home to the "Honfleur School", the *ferme* now provides luxury accommodation and a restaurant. *Rue Adolphe-Marais; 34 rooms; Tel. 02 31 89 23 61; Fax 02 31 89 48 48; category L*

Hostellerie Lechat

A venerable old hotel with a restaurant in the town centre. *Pl. Sainte-Catherine; 23 rooms; Tel. 02 31 14 49 49; Fax 02 31 89 28 61; category 1*

Hotel de la Tour

Near the harbour. A well-appointed, friendly hotel. *3, quai de la Tour; 48 rooms; Tel. 02 31 89 21 22; Fax 02 31 14 49 49; category 2*

ENTERTAINMENT

Visitors are soon captivated by the lively hustle and bustle at the *Vieux Bassin* and in the picturesque squares. If that's not loud enough for you, you can go and live it up at the *Black Jack* disco in the *Route Jean Revel* .

INFORMATION

Office de Tourisme
Rue de la Ville; Tel. 02 31 89 23 30; Fax 02 31 89 31 82

ALONG THE CÔTE FLEURIE

Trouville (103/D3)
★ While more modest in character than the chic Deauville on the other side of the river, Trouville (pop. 6,500) has its own pleasant charm. The old fishing port is now a popular bathing resort, but it still retains its original flair. Visitors can enjoy a stroll through the pretty Old Town, along the promenade with its venerable old villas and around the exclusive yachting marina. The municipal museum, *Musée de Trouville (daily 10 am–12 am and 2 pm–7 pm; admission 10 FF)*, in the *Villa Montebello* is most interesting, as is the *Aquarium écologique (daily 10 am–12 am and 2 pm–7 pm, in summer 10 am–7.30 pm; admission 30 FF)*. An enjoyable day can be spent by visiting the picturesque fish market in the morning, spending the day on the wide, sandy beach and going to *Le Louisiane Follies*, the unique Louisiana-style casino in the evening. 15 km. Hotels/restaurants: *Le Clos Saint-Gatien*, hotel in the château *St-Gatien-de-Bois; 53 rooms; Tel. 02 31 65 16 08; category 1. Mercure; place Foch; 80 rooms; Tel. 02 31 87 38 38; category 1. Relais de la Cahotte; 11, rue Victor Hugo; 32 rooms; Tel. 02 31 98 30 20; category 2*

Deauville (103/D3)
★ Whenever anyone talks about the Côte Fleurie they always en-

Deauville, elegant and chic: perfect for gamblers

thuse about Deauville (pop. 5,000). This chic seaside resort has an international flair and is popular with high society from all over the world. The outward expression of this is seen in the famous casino, luxury hotels, elegant boutiques and the Rolls Royces parked casually along the promenade. However, the great era of exclusiveness now seems to be a thing of the past. On the beach, the names of former stars and starlets are immortalised on the changing cubicles and gaped at by tourists – a last breath of fading glamour. The bathing resort is now trying to reinvent itself as a conference centre, to maintain its fame and glory as the high point of the Côte Fleurie. This explains the wide choice of exclusive sports, such as horse racing, polo, golf and sailing. Of course, you can also simply go to the fine, sandy beach to bathe. At the casino in the evening there is roulette and black jack, as well as shows. There are also three night clubs and numerous discos. 16 km

Restaurants: *Le Ciro's; Promenade des Blanches; Tel. 02 31 14 31 31; category 1. Le Spinnaker; 52, rue Mirabeau; Tel. 02 31 88 24 40; category 1.* Both restaurants have very fine menus. Hotels: *Ibis.* Pleasant hotel. *9, quai de la Marine; 95 rooms; Tel. 02 31 14 50 00; Fax 02 31 14 50 05; category 2. Normandy.* Luxury hotel rich in tradition. *38, rue Jean-Mermoz; 300 rooms; Tel. 02 31 98 66 22; Fax 02 31 98 66 23; category L*

Villers-sur-Mer (103/D4)
There is one bathing resort after another along this section of the coast, also known as *Corniche Normande.* The classic seaside resort of *Villers-sur-Mer* has a fine, sandy beach which is over 5 km long and a row of romantic Norman-style half-timbered buildings (19th century). The *Musée paléontologique,* with fossils from the nearby limestone cliffs, is worth a visit. *Daily 10 am–12.30 pm and 2 pm–7 pm; admission free.* 23 km

Vaches Noires (103/D4)
★ The "Black Cows" are actually impressive formations of dark brown marlaceous rocks scattered over the long beach. Access is along a footpath from Auberville. 26 km

Houlgate (103/D4)
Just outside the village there is a wonderful panoramic view of the Dives estuary and along the coast. The charming little spa is a classic example of the French seaside resort and is very popular with holiday-makers. 28 km. Hotel: *Du Centre.* Pleasant, centrally located hotel. *31, rue des Bains; 22 rooms; Tel. 02 31 24 80 40; Fax 02 31 28 52 21; category 2*

Dives-sur-Mer (103/D4)
The historic importance of this port (pop. 6,000) dates back to 1066 when William the Conqueror assembled his fleet here before his invasion of England. The wooden market halls (15th century) and a number of old houses (16th century) bear impressive witness to the mediaeval history of this former harbour town. The harbour has long since silted up. The original Romanesque church of *Notre-Dame* (11th–15th century) is also worth seeing. The *Village d'art Guillaume-le-Conquérant* provides excellent shopping facilities, with

elegant shops selling works of art, handicrafts and antiques. 30 km

Cabourg (103/D4)
★ Cabourg was a purpose-built holiday resort which was originally created on the drawing board in 1860. The result is that all roads lead straight to the casino. They are lined with houses which have the friendly charm of the *Belle Époque*. The *Promenade Marcel Proust* runs along the fine, sandy beach and commemorates the great novelist who, because of the climate, spent many years here living in the *Grand Hôtel*. The romantic seaside resort (pop. 3,000) has a great deal to offer holiday-makers. There are water sports, the yacht club, sailing schools and beach sailing, as well as evening entertainment in the casino, with its games of chance, theatre, cinema, night club and bars. 33 km

Merville-Franceville (103/D4)
The westernmost bathing resort on the *Côte Fleurie* is situated on the sandy estuary of the Orne. Its strategic importance is indicated by the *Redoute de Vauban*, a fortification dating from the 18th century. This was last used by the Germans as a defence base during the invasion of 1944. In the *Casemate N° 1* a wide selection of exhibits document the fateful events of that period. 39 km

ALONG THE CÔTE DE NACRE

Ouistreham-Riva-Bella (102/C4)
On the Orne estuary, at the heart of the Norman coastal region, lies the harbour town of Ouistreham (pop. 6,000). It is sometimes known as the "Gateway to France", as many ships from England arrive at the ferry port here. Ouistreham's attractions include the Romanesque church of *Saint-Samson* (12th century), and the stone tithe barn (15th century). The town has now joined up with neighbouring Riva-Bella, one of the most popular bathing resorts on the *Côte de Nacre* which begins here. *Information: Côte de Nacre Tourisme; 25, rue E. Belin, 14730 Lion-sur-Mer; Tel. 02 31 96 43 55.* 41 km from Bayeux. Hotel/restaurant: *Broche d'Argent; pl. Général-de-Gaulle; Tel. 02 31 97 12 16; Fax 02 31 97 03 33; category 2.* The *Château Bénouville* (18th century) is set in an extensive park above the Orne and is a good destination for an excursion. 10 km

Courseulles-sur-Mer (102/C3)
From *Riva-Bella* onwards there is one bathing resort after another. *Lion-sur-Mer, Luc-sur-Mer, Langrune-sur-Mer, Saint-Aubin-sur-Mer* and *Courseulles-sur-Mer* all have long, fine, sandy beaches which are wonderful for relaxing and bathing *en famille*. *Courseulles* with its former fishing harbour is a popular destination for boats and yachts, not least because of the famous oyster farm. 20 km from Bayeux.

Hotel/restaurant: *Ferme de la Rançonnière; Crépon, Route d'Arromanches; 35 rooms; Tel. 02 31 22 21 73; Fax 02 31 22 98 39; category 2*

Arromanches-les-Bains (102/B3)
During the invasion in 1944, this peaceful fishing village was one of the Allies' main landing places. In a daredevil operation, artificial breakwaters and landing stages

The seaside resort of Houlgate maintains its appeal to all ages

were towed here by sea and installed off the coast, enabling troops and thousands of tonnes of equipment to be landed to provide reinforcements for the next operations. In the *Musée du Débarquement* an exhibition gives an account of the landings. *Daily 9.30 am–6 pm; in summer until 7 pm; admission 32 FF.* In the *Cinema Arromanches 360*, a cinema in the round, visitors can see an 18-minute archive film which depicts the dramatic events of 1944. *Daily 10.10 am–4.40 pm; June–Aug 9 am, 10 am–6.40 pm; admission 22 FF.* 10 km from Bayeux

Omaha Beach (102/B3)
The whole length of the Côte de Nacre was used for the Allied landings during the invasion on 6 June 1944. The eastern section was used by the British and Canadian forces and includes *Sword Beach, Juno Beach* and *Gold Beach*, while the western section, including *Omaha Beach* and *Utah Beach*, was used by the American troops. The D-Day landings were a unique operation on a gigantic scale. Military cemeteries and museums, monuments and memorials, as well as the ruins of many massive bunker complexes, still bear witness today to the dramatic events of 1944. Today the wide, sandy beaches provide a paradise for sand sailors at low tide. 19 km from Bayeux

Pointe du Hoc (102/A3)
★ Just before Grandcamp-Maisy, the westernmost point on the Côte de Nacre famous for its coveted scallops, lies the rocky spur of the *Pointe du Hoc.* The spectacular headland was a strategic position used as a German observation point. During the landings it was the site of fierce fighting. 29 km from Bayeux

Along the coast through green countryside

A wild, windswept heath landscape, edged with strange rocky cliffs and gentle sandy beaches

With the fascinating *Cotentin* peninsula, the Département of Manche provides some lovely splashes of colour to the characteristic picture of rural Normandy. This is the land of open countryside, wonderful beaches and wind-whipped coastlines. The baren earth provides little nourishment and is only suitable as pasture land. The pastures are enclosed by windswept hedges and the moorland landscape is full of bushes and shrubs which provide a riot of colour when they bloom during the summer. In the sparsely populated inland region there are also wooded areas. The often steep, rugged north coast has a wild and exciting air. It is the very opposite of the east and west coasts where, to the delight of the holiday-makers, there are flat, sandy beaches. The sea is gradually retreating further than ever and the alluvial land in the *Baie du Mont Saint Michel* is threatening to silt up completely, much to the regret of the countless admirers of the famous holy rock. The salt plains help to make up for this with a culinary delicacy; the meat of the cows and sheep which graze this area is imbued with a fine aromatic flavour. Agriculture as a whole, but especially dairy produce, plays a very important role in the *Manche* region because, save for tourism which is beginning to flourish here, there are few other thriving employment sectors.

Exotic plants in the Jardin des Plantes in Avranches, formerly the convent garden of the Capucin Order

AVRANCHES

(101/D6, 106/C1) The ideal location of Avranches, on a hill above the *Baie du Mont Saint Michel*, played an important role from the very beginning in the fate of this historic town. In the 8th century the Bishop of Avranches founded *Mont Tombe*, the Benedictine abbey, on the famous rock, thus linking the turbulent history of Mont Saint Michel with Avranches for centuries. Because of the fertile land which surrounds it, the former diocesan town (pop. 8,700) is now an important centre of agricultural production, focusing mainly on sheep farming.

MARCO POLO SELECTION: MANCHE

1 Mont Saint Michel
The legendary abbey on the rock, one of Normandy's most impressive attractions (page 77)

2 Barfleur
Picturesque fishing port in the north-east corner of the Cotentin peninsula (page 74)

3 Martinvast
A lovely Norman fortification with ponds and waterfalls in the park (page 75)

4 Sainte-Mère-Église
Curious sight on the church tower (page 75)

5 Saint-Vaast-la-Hougue
Seaside fun in the waves and the culinary delight of fresh oysters (page 75)

6 Haras National
Stallions at the stud farm in Saint-Lô founded by Napoleon (page 79)

7 Abbaye Sainte Trinité
The abbey at Lessay in the midst of a fantastic heath landscape (page 81)

8 Avranches
The wonderful view from the *Jardin des Plantes* across the *Baie du Mont Saint Michel* (page 70)

SIGHTS

Donjon
The 13th-century keep, reinforced with battlements and machicolations, stands out from the ruins of the old fortifications. Behind the keep is the site of the destroyed cathedral and all around are the lovely mediaeval lanes of the historic Old Town which just beg to be explored.

Doyenné
The Dean's Palace (18th century) is just as impressive as the Palace of Justice (15th century), the former residence of the Bishop.

Jardin des Plantes
★ The former convent garden of the Capuchin Order has an impressive collection of exotic plants and flowers and also affords a breathtaking view across the picturesque bay and the rocky splendour of *Mont Saint Michel.*

Saint-Gervais
This church, with its 74-metre-high granite tower, is the symbol of the town. Inside, in the *Musée du Trésor de la Basilique St-Gervais,* visitors can admire a reliquary and a number of other valuable art treasures. *Daily except Tues 10 am–12 am and 2 pm–6 pm; Sun 2 pm–6 pm; admission 12 FF*

MUSEUMS

Bibliothèque du Fonds Ancien
The renowned Mont Saint Michel collection of precious manuscripts. *In the town hall; June–Aug daily except Tues 9.30 am–12 am and 2 pm–6 pm; admission 20 FF*

Musée Municipal

The former *Palais Episcopal* houses the municipal museum, with valuable manuscripts (8th–15th century) produced by the monks of Mont Saint Michel. *Pl. Jean de Saint-Avit; Apr–Sept daily except Tues 9.30 am–12 am and 2 pm–6 pm; admission 12 FF*

RESTAURANT

Jardin des Plantes

The restaurant serves good local fare in a pleasant atmosphere. *10, pl. Carnot; Tel. 02 33 58 03 68; category 2*

HOTEL

Les Abrincates

Distinctive hotel. *37, bd. du Luxembourg; 29 rooms; Tel. 02 33 58 66 64; Fax 02 33 58 40 11; category 2*

INFORMATION

Office de Tourisme

2, rue du Général de Gaulle; Tel. 02 33 58 00 22; Fax 02 33 68 13 29

SURROUNDING AREA

Ducey (101/D6, 106/C2)

It is well worth going on an excursion into the interesting countryside of the *Sélune* Valley carved deep into the granite. The best place to start is in the village of Ducey which, during Roman times, was a strategic river crossing protected by a castle. Two reservoirs at *La Roche-qui-Boit* and *Vézins* have formed lakes which are very popular with water sports enthusiasts. As well as canoeists, anglers also enjoy their sport along the Sélune and its tributaries. 11 km

Granville (100/C5)

The popular seaside resort (pop. 15,600) is situated on a slate outcrop which projects into the sea, marking the end of the *Baie du Mont Saint Michel*. This is where the greatest tidal differences in Europe are recorded – up to 14 m. Perched on top of the rock is the granite-grey *Haute Ville*, surrounded by a fortified wall. Note the church of *Notre Dame* (15th– 17th century) in the Old Town. The fortified gateway *Grande Porte* is also interesting. It houses the *Musée du Vieux Granville (2, rue Lecarpentier; daily except Tues 10 am–12 am and 2 pm–6 pm; admission 10 FF)* which has exhibitions of regional and local history. The town also boasts numerous venerable old town houses (16th–18th century). A walk around the town walls affords panoramic views of the harbour, coast and sea. There is a lovely cliff path to the *Pointe du Roc*, where there is a lighthouse. In the *Basse Ville* there is the ferry and fishing port with restaurants serving fresh seafood. 26 km. Restaurant: *Le Phare; 11, rue Port; Tel. 02 33 50 12 94; category 2.* Hotels: *Des Bains; 19, rue Clémenceau; 49 rooms; Tel. 02 33 50 17 31; Fax 02 33 50 89 22; category 1–2. Le Herel; Port de Plaisance; 43 rooms; Tel. 02 33 90 48 08; Fax 02 33 90 75 95; category 2*

Iles Chausey (100/C5)

The group of islands called the *Iles Chausey* are reached after a 55-minute boat journey from Granville. At high tide fifty islands are visible but at low tide it is 350. The largest one is *Grande Ile* which is inhabited by fishermen. In the coastal waters there are lobsters and shrimps, in the air a noisy seabird paradise. 16 km from Granville

The Grande Ile is the only island of the Iles Chausey which can be visited

Mortain (101/E6, 107/D2)
On a gentle hill in the middle of the enchanting countryside of the *Bocage Mortainais* is the holiday resort of *Mortain* (pop. 3,000). Back in Norman times the town was fortified. The Cistercian convent, the *Abbaye Blanche* (12th century) is now used as a centre of spirituality. Visitors can see the church, chapterhouse, cellar and the remains of a Romanesque cloister with lovely round-arched arcades; *June–Sept daily except Tues 9 am–11.45 am and 2.30 pm–5.30 pm.* Outside the historic town, in the valley of the *Cance*, is the *Grande Cascade*, a waterfall which tumbles furiously over granite scree for 25 metres. Nearby is the 35-metre-high *Petite Cascade*. 32 km

Villedieu-les-Poêles (101/D-E5)
This little town was founded in the 11th century by the Knights Hospitallers of Malta. It is situated in the *Sienne Valley* which is famous for its trout. However, it was not the fish but the coppersmiths and later the bell-founders who turned the town (pop. 5,000) in the *Bocage* into the legendary *Cité du cuivre*. Today visitors can still see one bell-foundry and a few workshops where copper saucepans, pots and various other metal utensils are produced. *Fonderie de Cloches Atelier Cormille-Havard; rue du Pont Chignon; daily 8 am–12 am and 2 pm–5.30 pm. Atelier du Cuivre; 54, rue du Général Huard; daily 9 am–12 am and 2 pm–6.30 pm.* The stone church of *Notre-Dame* (15th century) has an interesting lantern tower over the crossing. 22 km. Hotels: *Manoir de l'Acherie; Sainte-Cécile; 14 rooms; Tel. 02 33 51 13 87; Fax 02 33 61 89 07; category 2–3. St-Pierre et St-Michel; 12, pl. de la République; 23 rooms; Tel. 02 33 61 00 11; Fax 02 33 61 06 52; category 2*

CHERBOURG

(101/D1) This traditional harbour town (pop. 90,000) still maintains its naval prestige, with many mighty ocean-going steamers docking here. The famous liner, Queen Elizabeth II, comes here five times a year amid great ceremony. But Cherbourg is also popular with yachters, and ferries serve the port daily. Cherbourg was founded as a harbour and commercial centre and the town has always been full of lively activity both at sea and on land. During the Hundred Years' War there were strong fortifications here which were then destroyed at the end of the 17th century. The military engineer, Sébastien Vauban recognised the excellent strategic position of this town on the north coast of the *Cotentin*. In 1853, his idea was finally taken up and, using his plans, the dam was constructed. The naval port was officially opened by Napoleon III in 1858. Cherbourg's great naval tradition remains unbroken as it is still home to France's third largest naval base. It is no surprise that the economic importance of the town is characterised by the shipyards and the metal industry and that Cherbourg was badly damaged during World War II. It was subsequently rebuilt, but the opportunity was wasted so that Cherbourg is now a modern town which is not especially attractive.

SIGHTS

Abbaye du Voeu

The abbey was founded in 1145 and the community remained here until 1774. The abbey suffered major war damage but this has now been repaired. Visitors can see the refectory and the gardens. *Rue de l'Abbaye*

Bassin du Commerce

The oldest part of the harbour area (1831) is the restored Old Town. The streets of the *Quartier des Halles* are wonderful for strolling through, hunting out a bargain and, of course, enjoying the local cuisine. Not far from here is the international yachting marina, *Chantereyne*, and the kilometre-long bathing beach.

Fort du Roule

The 19th-century fort is built at the top of the 112-metre-high *Montagne de Roule* on the south-eastern side of Cherbourg and affords a panoramic view over the rooftops and the extensive harbour.

Parc Emmanuel Liais

The gardens boast impressive collections of exotic plants. *22, rue de la Bucaille; daily except Mon 10 am–12 am and 2 pm–5 pm; admission 10 FF*

Sainte-Trinité

Anyone with a fondness for unusual churches should be sure not to miss the basilica of *Sainte-Trinité* (14th/15th century) which is built in the Flamboyant Gothic style. The splendid tower was added in the 19th century. *Daily 8 am–7 pm*

MUSEUMS

Musée de la Libération

The *Fort du Roule* has a collection of interesting documents and displays relating to the 1944 invasion. *Apr–Sept daily 10 am–6 pm, Oct–Mar daily except Mon 9.30 am–12 am and 2 pm–5.30 pm; admission 20 FF*

Musée Thomas-Henry

The museum has an excellent collection of European paintings

(15th–19th century), with works by Fra Angelico, Filippo Lippi and Jean-François Millet. *Centre Culturel; daily except Mon 9 am–12 am and 2 pm–6 pm; admission 15 FF*

RESTAURANT

Chez Pain
A pleasant restaurant which serves good fish dishes. *59, rue au Blé; Tel. 02 33 93 52 02; category 3*

HOTELS

Chantereyne
The hotel is by the harbour and has a view of the sea. *Port de Plaisance; 50 rooms; Tel. 02 33 93 02 20; Fax 02 33 93 45 29; category 2*

Liberté
Good hotel with an equally good restaurant. *Rue G. Sorel; 73 rooms; Tel. 02 33 43 72 00; Fax 02 33 20 01 32; category 2*

Mercure
Modern accommodation with a view of the marina. *Gare Maritime; 84 rooms; Tel. 02 33 44 01 11; Fax 02 33 44 51 00; category 2*

SPORTS & LEISURE

With 1,500 moorings, *Chantereyne* is the second largest yachting marina in France and consequently it is host to a wide range of popular, major international events. *Capitainerie du Port; Tel. 02 33 87 65 70; Fax 02 33 53 21 12*

ENTERTAINMENT

The wheel keeps spinning until the early hours in the *Casino* at the *Bassin du Commerce.*

INFORMATION

Maison du Tourisme
2, quai Alexandre III; Tel. 02 33 93 52 02; Fax 02 33 53 66 97

SURROUNDING AREA

Barfleur **(101/E1, 102/A1)**
★ A picturesque fishing port with extensive mussel beds along the coast. The lively town is popular with yachting enthusiasts. At the end of the harbour, on a massive rocky outcrop, is the defensive-looking church of *Saint-Nicolas* (17th century). 27 km. 2 km along the coast road is the *Pointe de Barfleur*, the north-eastern tip of the Cotentin, which has a 75-m-high lighthouse (1834). Next to it is the old lighthouse (a mere 20 m high).

Beaumont-Hague **(100/C1)**
In the middle of the barren landscape of the *Hague*, on a plain of about 300 ha, is the masive Beaumont nuclear complex, used for electricity generation. Further south, in *Flamanville*, there is another nuclear power station. Both complexes can be visited by appointment. *(Comega, Etablissement de la Hague; Apr–Sept daily 10 am–7 pm; Tel. 02 33 02 61 04).* 21 km

Bricquebec **(101/D2)**
This is a romantic little town with a remarkable château (13th century) which has been very well preserved. The 22-m-high, eleven-sided *donjon* (14th century) and the circular walls are particularly impressive. The underground chapel (13th century) has been lovingly restored. The clock tower houses a small art

museum *(in summer daily except Tues 10 am–12 am and 2 pm–6.30 pm; otherwise by appointment; Tel. 02 33 52 21 13; admission 7 FF)* and a highly recommended hotel. The *Abbaye Notre-Dame-de-Grâce* is inhabited by Trappists, a community which emerged from the Cistercian order. The *Abbaye* may only be viewed from the outside; *daily 3.30 pm information.* 18 km. Hotel/restaurant: *Vieux Château; 4, cours du Château; 20 rooms; Tel. 02 33 52 24 49; Fax 02 33 52 62 71; category 2*

Martinvast (101/D1)
★ Now listed among France's *Monuments Historiques*, the *Château Martinvast* was originally built as a Norman fortification. The parts of the château (11th–16th century) which still survive today include the *donjon.* In addition, the ponds and waterfalls in the English park are worth seeing. *In summer 2 pm–7 pm; otherwise weekends 2 pm–6 pm; admission 30 FF.* 6 km

Saint-Germain-des-Vaux (100/C1)
The small, wind-lashed village is situated near the rock formations of the *Cap de la Hague.* The big lighthouse marks the north-westernmost point of the Cotentin. In the village itself the *Jardin Jacques Prévert* contains interesting and rare tree species. 28 km

Sainte-Mère-Église (101/E3)
★ The first town to be liberated in 1944. A British paratrooper got caught on the church tower (11th–15th century) and a model of him hangs there today, a popular subject for photographs. The story of the landing is illustrated in the *Musée des Troupes Aéroportées; Pl. du 6 juin; daily 10 am–*

Sainte-Mère-Église

12 am and 2 pm–6 pm; admission 20 FF. 41 km

Saint-Pierre-Église (101/E1)
A quiet town with a large market place and a *château* (18th century). 19 km. Restaurant: *Au Bouquet de Cosqueville*; a well-kept secret on the way to the beach. *category 1*

Saint-Vaast-la-Hougue (101/E2)
★ The importance of the little fishing village (pop. 2,500), now famous for its oyster beds, dates back to 1694 after the battle of Hougue, where the French had suffered defeat at the hands of the English. At this point the fortifications and the harbour were rebuilt. The powerful *fort* (17th century), with its 16-m-thick central tower and the 3-m-thick walls bear witness to the art of fortress building. Thus protected, the seaside town was able to develop over the centuries without being destroyed. The sandy beach and the mild climate led to it becoming a popular bathing resort. 28 km

Saint-Vaast-la-Hougue attracts holiday-makers with its mild climate

Hotels/Restaurants: *Hôtel de France et des Fuchsias; 18, rue du Maréchal-Foch; 32 rooms; Tel. 02 33 54 42 26; Fax 02 33 43 46 79; category 2–3. La Granitière; 64, rue du Maréchal-Foch; 10 rooms; Tel. 02 33 54 58 99; Fax 02 33 20 34 91; category 1–2*

About 1 km out to sea is the *Ile de Tatihou* on which there stands a compact 18th century fortress. The island is popular with a large number of species of birds. A boat trip from the harbour is definitely worthwhile. Information: *Accueil Tatihou; Quai Vauban, 50550 Saint-Vaast-la-Hougue; Tel. 02 33 23 19 92; Fax 02 33 54 33 47*

Tourlaville **(101/D1)**

The elegant Italian Renaissance-style *château* (16th century) is surrounded by beautiful grounds with some splendid summer houses (19th century). Palms and flowers give the park a southern feeling. *The park is open daily 10 am–12 am and 2 pm–5 pm; in summer until 6 pm; admission free.* 3 km

Urville-Nacqueville **(101/D1)**

This Renaissance château (16th century) lies in a valley. It has an impressive façade and a park laid out in the English style. In the middle of this is the photogenic gatehouse (16th century). *Easter to 30 Sept daily except Tues and Thurs; admission 25 FF.* 10 km

Utah Beach **(101/E3, 102/A3)**

The Allies landed here during *Operation Overlord.* The *US-Memorial*, situated right by the sea, commemorates the spectacular landing in 1944 which led to the liberation of France. 43 km

Valognes **(101/D2)**
The "Norman Versailles" (pop. 7,000) at the heart of the *Cotentin* peninsula lost its beautiful Old Town in 1944. However, there is still evidence of Valogne's long and turbulent history extending as far back as Roman times. Thus, there are Gallo-Roman ruins and churches ranging from the 11th–18th centuries. The places of interest are all quite close together. There is the town house, the *Hôtel de Beaumont* (18th century), with its impressive façade, the *Hôtel de Grandval-Caligny* (17th–18th century) and the *Maison du Grand Quartier* (15th century), in which the *Musée Regional du Cidre* illustrates the five-hundred-year history of Normandy's famous beverage. *Apr–Sept except Wed daily 10 pm–12 am and 2 pm–6 pm; admission 20 FF.* 20 km

MONT SAINT MICHEL

☛ **City Map inside back cover**

(101/D6, 106/B2) ★ The legendary "mystical sacred rock of the Western world" is one of the most famous architectural monuments in France and the celebrated symbol of Normandy. The abbey perches on a huge lump of granite in the *Baie du Mont Saint Michel.* Towering 150 m above the sea, it can be seen from miles around. In the Middle Ages the indescribable spell cast by Mont Saint Michel attracted thousands of pilgrims. Now it holds the same fascination for millions of tourists. Approaching it across the 1.5-km-long causeway, each step reveals a constantly changing image, as the sky, air and sea play on the enthralling spectacle ahead. The water began to retreat from the massive rock long ago and the Bay is gradually starting to silt up. It is only at the equinoxes that it is once again surrounded by water. Legend has it that Bishop Aubert of Avranches was charged by the Archangel Michael in 708 to build a chapel on the *Mont Tombe.* In 966 the Benedictine monastery was then founded and over the ensuing centuries one religious building after another was built here, one on top of the other. In 1897 the building on the rock was finally completed when a gilt statue of the Archangel Michael was put on the pinnacle of the church.

SIGHTS

As you approach Mont Saint Michel you will become caught up in the streams of visitors. Both near the entrance at the *Porte de l'Avancée* and on the *Grande Rue* leading up to the abbey there is a constant hustle and bustle. Shops, souvenir stalls, crêperies and restaurants result in long queues which can become unbearable unless you concentrate on the picturesque mediaeval backdrop. It is only as you begin the rather strenuous ascent up the steep flights of steps to the abbey itself that the crowds begin to thin out. On the way up you will pass the fortified walls, towers and terraces which afford a wonderful view of the magnificent religious architecture as you draw closer to it. Passing the buildings which are lived in by the monks who still inhabit the abbey, you will eventually reach the *Terrasse de l'Ouest.* This is the departure point for guided tours which take visitors around the abbey buildings. These include the abbey church (11th century), the crypts, the Gothic abbey building, *La Merveille*, with the single-naved refectory and the four-aisled Knights Hall, meeting place of the Order of Saint Michael. The high point is the extraordinary cloister, built as a place of peace and meditation. The beautiful pointed-arched arcading, decorated with Norman ornamentation, rests on pairs of slim pillars. In the *Salles des Hôtesses*, beneath the cloister, the Abbot would once have welcomed and entertained rich and important guests, while the almonry was used to receive pilgrims and to dispense alms to the poor. Returning to the west terrace, the wealth of impressions with which Mont Saint Michel entrances its visitors is finally completed with a fantastic, panoramic view of the bay, the coast and the sea.

May–Sept daily 9 am–5.30 pm, Oct–Apr 9.30 am–4.30 pm; 37 FF

MUSEUM

L'Archéoscope
Multimedia show (25 mins) about the history and legends of Mont Saint Michel. *Grande Rue; daily 9 am–6 pm; admission 30 FF*

RESTAURANTS

Chapeau Blanc
In the hotel Saint Pierre. Good cuisine in a pleasant atmosphere. *Grande Rue; Tel. 02 33 60 14 03; category 2*

La Mère Poulard
It would be unforgivable to go to Mont Saint Michel without sampling the famous omelettes served by this restaurant. *Grande Rue; Tel. 02 33 60 14 01; category 1*

HOTELS

Relais du Roy
On the mainland at the end of the causeway, making it a little less disturbed by the hustle and bustle of the tourists up on the rock itself. *27 rooms; Digue, D 976; Tel. 02 33 60 14 25; Fax 02 33 60 37 69; category 2*

Saint-Pierre
Mediaeval half-timbered building. Well-appointed rooms and friendly service. There is a good restaurant as well. *21 rooms; Grande Rue; Tel. 02 33 48 59 82; Fax 02 33 48 59 82; category 1*

INFORMATION

Office de Tourisme
Tel. 02 33 60 14 30;
Fax 02 33 60 06 75

SAINT-LÔ

(101/E4, 102/A4) High up on a striking rock, with the beautiful Vire Valley down below, is the Département capital of Saint-Lô (pop. 25,000). During World War II, Saint-Lô was almost completely destroyed and many of the beautiful features of this town, which was founded in the 6th century, were lost. Unfortunately the rebuilding of the Saint-Lô was not entirely successful. However, the old town walls and the church were restored with great care and skill, making a visit worthwhile. Saint-Lô is now an important agricultural centre and the famous stud farm here helps to attract plenty of visitors to the town.

SIGHTS

Haras National

★ To the east of the town is the stud farm, *Haras National*, which was founded in 1806 by Napoléon Bonaparte and enjoys a great deal of prestige in France. Visitors are welcome to come and admire more than 100 well-looked-after stallions standing in their stables. *Av. du Maréchal Juin; in summer daily 2 pm–5 pm, otherwise weekends only 2 pm–5 pm; admission 20 FF*

Notre-Dame

In the heart of the town is the church of *Notre-Dame* (13th–17th century), built in the Flamboyant style. The church also suffered during World War II. However, the restoration has revealed the building in all its former glory again and emphasises the elegant and airy chancel aisles.

Old town walls

It is well worth strolling round the walls. The old fortified enclosure is dominated by a massive tower from which there is a wonderful panoramic view over the Vire valley and the countryside of the *Bocage.*

MUSEUM

Musée Municipal des Beaux-Arts

Art museum in the town hall with valuable 16th/17th century tapestries. There are also paintings by Eugène Boudin, Camille Corot and Jean-François Millet (18th/19th century). *Pl. du Champ de Mars; daily except Tues 10 am–12 am and 2 pm–6 pm; admission 10 FF*

RESTAURANT

Le Tocqueville

This little restaurant has a pleasant atmosphere and boasts ex-

Parc Naturel Régional des Marais du Cotentin et du Bessin

The marshland area of the Cotentin and Bessin is a magnificent nature reserve containing a rich diversity of the flora and fauna of Normandy. The flat swampy areas are surrounded by the sea and during the winter months they are flooded. It is only in the spring, when the water begins to recede, that the meadows, full of rushes and sedges, can be used as grazing land for horses, cows and sheep. The marshland region can be explored by going on boat trips along the Douvre and the Taute, as well as on lake trips in the Baie des Veys. In addition, you can go on an excursion by horse and cart.

Information from the *Parc Naturel Régional des Marais du Cotentin et du Bessin; Manoir de Cantepie, 50500 Les Veys; Tel. 02 33 71 61 90; Fax 02 33 71 61 91*

cellent cuisine. *Pl. de la Gare; Tel. 02 33 05 08 63; category 3*

HOTELS

Relais Mercure
Opposite the town walls, not far from the centre. Friendly hotel. *1, av. Briovère; 34 rooms; Tel. 02 33 05 10 84; Fax 02 33 56 46 92; category 2*

Les Voyageurs
Simple, reasonably-priced hotel. *5/7, av. Briovère; Tel. 02 33 05 08 63; Fax 02 33 05 14 34; category 3*

INFORMATION

Office de Tourisme
Pl. du Général de Gaulle; Tel. 02 33 05 02 09; Fax 02 33 05 26 08

SURROUNDING AREA

Barneville-Carteret (100/C2-3)
Shielded from the breakers by the Channel Islands and gently washed by the Gulf Stream, this popular bathing resort (pop. 2,500) has a mild, temperate climate. Clean, sandy beaches with high dunes attract plenty of holiday-makers. Excursions to the Channel Islands leave from the harbour daily. In the centre of Barneville is the Romanesque parish church (11th century) with decorative capitals. The *Rue du Cap* goes out to the lighthouse on the *Cap de Carteret*, a good starting point for long walks along the beach and the cliff tops. 30 km from Cherbourg

Restaurant: *Le Gohan.* This former barn retains a historical atmosphere. Serves good fish and grilled dishes. *Rue au Lait; Tel. 02 33 04 95 33; category 2*

Hotel: *La Marine; 11, rue de Paris; 31 rooms; Tel. 02 33 53 83 31; Fax 02 33 53 39 60; category 2*

Carentan (101/E3)
The old diocesan town, often known as the *Gateway to the Cotentin*, is situated in the *Baie des Veys*. All around there are large tracts of marshland and pasture which have made the little town (pop. 7,000) into a centre for dairy produce. Every Monday there is a big cattle market. In the middle of this attractive town is the Gothic cathedral of *Notre-Dame* (11th–16th century), with its octagonal belltower. Another place of interest is the town hall (17th century), which is in a former convent, and a row of stone houses with very impressive Gothic arcades (15th century). 28 km

Hotel: *Aire de la Baie; R.N. 13, Les Veys; 40 rooms; Tel. 02 33 42 00 99; Fax 02 33 71 06 94; category 2*

Cerisy-la-Forêt (101/F4, 102/A4)
The Benedictine abbey of *Saint-Vigor* was founded in the 6th century. Parts of the abbey building have survived, as has the interesting church (11th century) which is among the most beautiful Romanesque buildings in Normandy. The small museum displays statues and wall and floor tiles which date back to the 14th and 15th centuries. *Easter–15 Nov daily 9 am–6.30 pm; admission 15 FF.* 15 km

Coutances (101/D4)
Above the Rivers *Prépont* and *Bulsard*, built on a gentle hill, Coutances (pop. 13,000) enjoyed great prestige for many centuries

as the secret capital of the *Cotentin.* The town owed its position largely to the fine cathedral of *Notre-Dame* (13th/15th century) erected on the highest point. With its two lofty spires and the massive crossing tower, the building is an impressive example of the Norman Gothic style. Other places of interest are the town hall, which has a lovely façade, and the terraced botanical garden, the *Jardin des Plantes.* 27 km

Hotel: *Cositel; Route de Coutainville; 55 rooms; Tel. 02 33 07 51 64; Fax 02 33 07 06 23; category 2–3*

A pleasant excursion can be made to the nearby *Château de Gratot* (14th–16th century). The powerful building with its four imposing towers is surrounded by a wide moat. *Daily 9 am – 7 pm*

Hambye **(101/D5)**
Nestling in the romantic Seine Valley, to start with the *Abbaye de Hambye* (12th century) enjoyed a peaceful existence. However, the Early Gothic building was seized during the French Revolution and afterwards all that remained were ruins. The remains of the abbey give an idea of the huge scale and splendour of this former Benedictine abbey. *Daily except Tues 10 am–12 am and 2 pm–6 pm; admission 20 FF.* 27 km

Lessay **(101/D3)**
★ Right in the middle of a fantastic heath landscape is the little town of Lessay (pop. 14,000), which is rich in tradition. The high point is the Benedictine abbey, the *Abbaye Sainte-Trinité* (11th century), with its Romanesque ribbed vaults. *Daily 8 am–7 pm; admission free.* 36 km. The surrounding marshland of *Mathon* is an impressive nature reserve. Nature lovers can enjoy a walk here and the chance to see rare plants and insects.

Portbail **(100/C3)**
This popular bathing resort (pop. 17,000) marks the beginning of kilometres of fine, sandy beaches, lined with dunes. There is a busy yachting marina and in the summer ferries go from here to the Channel Islands. By the harbour is the fortified church of *Notre-Dame* (11th century) which has lovely capitals of Romanesque origin. 58 km

Saint-Sauveur-le-Vicomte **(101/D3)**
This fortified town, important during the Hundred Years' War, is at the heart of the *Cotentin* peninsula. Of the *château* (11th century), the encircling walls, prison tower and square keep have survived. The destruction of 1944 has been extensively repaired. To the south is the Romanesque Benedictine abbey. In 1832 it became the mother house of the Order of the Sisters of Charity. *Daily 10 am–12 am and 2.30 pm–5 pm; admission free.* 55 km

Troisgots-la-Chapelle-sur-Vire **(101/D3)**
This place of pilgrimage has been a well-known and popular destination since the 12th century. The chapel houses the unforgettable statue of *Notre-Dame-de-Vire* (15th century). Another feature which attracts the visitors is the imposing *Château Angotière* (16th–18th century) on the southern edge of the village. It has a splendid park. 14 km

The harmony of nature in a hilly landscape

Woodland, hedges, meadows and lakes merge harmoniously to create a unique garden landscape

Although the steep cliffs and sandy beaches of Normandy exert a seemingly magnetic attraction on countless tourists, this is not all the region has to offer. Normandy also has a unique inland area which is a real paradise for holiday-makers who prefer the peace and quiet of the countryside. *Suisse Normande* in the north, the *Parc Naturel Régional Normandie-Maine* in the south and *Perche* in the centre of the region are all landscapes which have their own distinctive characters. This hilly area, with its trees, hedges and small lakes, is dominated by large tracts of woodland, from *Reno-Valdieu* in the east to *Bellême, Saint-Evroult, Ecouves, Andaine* and *Halouze* in the west. *Orne* too has a rich pattern of magnificent castle grounds and parks, providing an ideal environment for the horses which are bred in the many stud farms here.

The Orne countryside is perfect for riders and walkers

Thus, *Orne* presents nature-lovers with a unique garden landscape.

ALENÇON

(108/A3) At Normandy's southern extreme, on the edge of the *Parc Naturel Régional Normandie-Maine*, is the capital of the Département of Orne. *Alençon* (pop. 35,000) is surrounded by extensive forest and is consequently a good starting point for a wide range of wonderful walks – from *Perseigne* to the area around *Andaine*, from *Ecouves* as far as the *Alpes Mancelles*. The town is the centre of a region shaped by agriculture. However, it also became an important industrial and commercial centre. Over the last few centuries, the former ducal seat made a name for itself with the production of the famous *Point d'Alençon* lace. Alençon was badly damaged during World War II, but the historic heart of the town, with its half-timbered buildings, has been restored.

SIGHTS

Château des Ducs
In the *Place Foch* the gatehouse of the seigneurial château (15th century) which was slighted by Jean I and Jean II still stands. Flanked by two massive towers it watches over what is now a prison.

Maison d'Ozé
This 15th century palace is one of the town's most valuable architectural monuments. It now houses the *Office de Tourisme* and an exhibition about the history of the town. *Pl. Lamagdelaine; daily 9 am–6.30 pm*

Notre-Dame
The original Romanesque church of *Notre-Dame* in the town centre was built in the 15th century in the lovely Flamboyant Gothic style. The magnificent portal is an impressive masterpiece. The tower, crossing, transept and chancel were sensitively restored after a fire in the 18th century. Note the 16th-century windows. *Pl. Lamagdelaine; Mon–Sat 9 am–12 am and 2 pm–6 pm, Sun 9 am–12 am and 2 pm–5 pm*

Saint-Léonard
At the heart of Alençon is the lovely Old Town district of *Saint-Léonard.* Its pretty little lanes with their lovely mediaeval half-timbered buildings are so inviting. Visitors can admire a wide range of attractive façades, windows and wrought iron balcony balustrades. Don't miss the church of *Saint-Léonard* (15th century).

MUSEUMS

Musée de la Dentelle au Point d'Alençon
★ The lace museum illustrates how the famous *Point d'Alençon* lace was made. There is also a display of all the different sorts of French lace. *31, rue du Pont-Neuf; daily except Sun and holidays 10 am–12 am and 2 pm–6 pm; admission 20 FF*

MARCO POLO SELECTION: ORNE

1 **Point d'Alençon**
Exquisite hand-made lace in the two Musées de la Dentelle in Alençon (pages 84 and 85)

2 **Château d'O**
Graceful moated château at Mortrée (page 87)

3 **Le Pin-au-Haras**
The famous stud farm which exerts a magnetic attraction on all horse lovers (page 86)

4 **Saint-Céneri-le-Gérei**
One of France's 100 most beautiful villages with a particularly beautiful Romanesque church (page 87)

5 **Sées Cathedral**
The cathedral on the banks of the River Orne is considered to be a masterpiece of High Gothic architecture (page 87)

Musée des Beaux-Arts et de la Dentelle
★ Works by French painters (17th–20th century) and displays of hand-made lace. *12, rue Charles-Avelin; daily except Mon 10 pm–12 am and 2 pm–6 pm; admission 16 FF*

RESTAURANT

L'Escargot Doré
Excellent, regional cuisine. *183, av. du Général Leclerc; Tel. 02 33 28 67 67; category 2*

SHOPPING

Of course, there are plenty of opportunities to purchase souvenirs in the lace town. But be careful: if an item is cheap, it cannot be genuinely hand-made. Lace bought from museums is authentic.

HOTEL

Le Grand Cerf
Good accommodation with a reasonable restaurant. *21, rue Saint-Blaise; 20 rooms; Tel. 02 33 26 00 51; Fax 02 33 26 63 07; category 2*

ENTERTAINMENT

✝ Disco at the *L'Arc en Ciel; 11, rue de la Halle aux Toiles;* and live music at *La Luciole; 171, rue de Bretagne*

INFORMATION

Office de Tourisme
Maison d'Ozé; Tel. 02 33 26 11 36; Fax 02 33 32 10 53

SURROUNDING AREA

Argentan (108/A2, 103/D6)
This town on the *Orne* (pop. 18,000) also made its name through lace-making. In the exhibition entitled *Le Point d'Argentan* the old traditions are still preserved and visitors can watch lace-makers at work. *Daily except Mon 10 am – 12 am and 2 pm – 6 pm; admission 10 FF.* During World War II, Argentan suffered major destruction and the restoration work deserves a special mention. This is particularly true of the two Flamboyant-style churches: *Saint-Germain* (15th–17th century) and *Saint-Martin* (15th–16th century). All that remains of the mediaeval château are the ruins of the *donjon* (12th century). 44 km

Bellême (108/B4)
The historic old town (pop. 1,800) is situated on a hill above the *Forêt de Bellême,* which is a lovely place for walking. In the past, Bellême, as a ducal seat, formed the focal point of *Perche.* Nowadays it is the ruins of the fortifications, the gatehouse flanked by towers (15th century), the church of *Saint-Sauveur* (15th–17th century) and the lovely town houses (17th/18th century) which attract the tourists. Particularly popular among the ancient little lanes is the charming *Rue Ville-Close.* 41 km

Carrouges (107/F2)
The *Château de Carrouges* (14th–17th century) lies in a park, surrounded by a moat. It is surely one of Normandy's most beautiful châteaux. The styles and building materials span three centuries, giving Carrouges its own unique appeal. Note the *donjon* (14th century) and the graceful gatehouse (16th century), with its saddle roof and round towers. *Daily 10 am–*

11.30 am and 2 pm–5.30 pm; admission 32 FF. 29 km

Domfront (107/E2)
135 m up above the *Varenne Valley* is the little mediaeval town of Domfront (pop. 4,500) which is full of history. The once-powerful fortress (11th century) was razed in 1608 by Henry IV. The remains nestle in the grass of the park and, with the towers from the old town walls, exude a tranquil atmosphere. The historic character of the mediaeval town is also accentuated by the narrow lanes and charming half-timbered houses. The Romanesque church of *Notre-Dame-sur-l'Eau* (11th/12th century) is a fine example of Norman architecture, *daily 9 am–6 pm*. 61 km

Le Pin-au-Haras (108/A2)
★ The *château* (18th century) which belongs to the *Haras du Pin*

The Château d'O near Mortrée and not far from Sées

stud farm is imbued with a simple, impressive elegance. Although the château is closed to the public, the stables and horseshoe-shaped courtyard of the famous stud farm can be visited. *Apr – Oct daily 9.30 am–6 pm, at other times daily 10 am–12 am and 2 pm–5 pm; admission 25 FF.* 38 km

Mortagne-au-Perche (108/B3)
The quiet capital of *Perche* (pop. 5,000) lies in a fertile landscape of which there is a magnificent view from the *Jardin Public.* The centrepiece of the town is the Flamboyant-style *Église Notre-Dame* which dates from the 15th century. It has an impressive tower. Inside there is some fine 18th-century wooden panelling. Another high point is the beautiful cloister in the *Hôpital Hospice*, a former Franciscan foundation. However, Mortagne also owes its fame to its reputation as "Black pudding capital" and the delicacy should certainly be sampled, ideally at the popular Black Pudding Market. 31 km

Mortrée (108/A2)
An excursion to the extraordinarily charming ★ *Château d'O* (15th–17th century) is a must. The famous Renaissance château is built in the Flamboyant style and is surrounded on all sides by a wide moat, creating an unforgettable impression. *Daily except Tues 2.30 pm–5 pm, in summer 10 am – 12 am and 2 pm – 6 pm; admission 30 FF.* 25 km

Only 4 km away from here, on the edge of the wooded region of *Ecouves*, is the village of *Saint-Christophe-le-Jajolet* with the elegant *Château de Sassy* (18th century). The park and the terraced gardens which are laid out in the French style are rightly famed for their beauty. *Apr–Oct daily 3 pm–6 pm; park open all year round; admission 25 FF*

Saint-Céneri-le-Gérei (108/B2)
★ The picturesque village is situated above a loop in the Sarthe and announces proudly that it is "One of France's 100 most beautiful villages." This is partly because of the lovely view of the ridges of the *Alpes Mancelles*, but also because of the countless little lanes, an ancient bridge and, the crowning glory, the little Romanesque church, one of Normandy's finest. It dates from 1050. The apse has two chapels and the tower is tropped with a saddle roof. The banks of the Sarthe are a great place for angling. 14 km

Sées (108/A2)
★ The ancient little diocesan town (4th century) on the River Orne has a population of 5,000. It is dominated by the great cathedral of *Notre-Dame* (13th century). The cathedral had a turbulent history and is a masterpiece of the Norman High Gothic style. *Daily 9 am–6.30 pm.* 21 km

Hotel: *Le Dauphin; 32, pl. des Halles; 7 rooms; Tel. 02 33 27 8 07; Fax 02 33 28 80 33; category 2*

Soligny-la-Trappe (108/C3)
In the hilly countryside of *Perche*, in the little village of *Soligny*, is a Cistercian monastery (12th century). It illustrates very vividly the history of the Trappists. The *Abbaye* (19th century) is not usually open to the public but all manner of monastery products are sold here which justifies a visit. 45 km

Tours around Normandy

These routes are marked in green on the map on the inside front cover and in the Road Atlas beginning on page 100

① ALONG THE SEINE VALLEY TO THE SEA

Anyone planning to travel to Normandy from Paris will take the A 13 motorway to Rouen. This is certainly the quickest route. However, should you wish to take the more scenic route, you should leave the motorway half way to Rouen and then follow the path of the Seine on its way to the sea. The route boasts an endless series of unique sights; in the river's many loops you can explore any number of historic highlights and beautiful landscapes. Day trip: around 140 km to the sea.

Leave the A 13 motorway at Exit 16 going in the direction of *Vernon (p. 51)*. On the edge of the little mediaeval town is the interesting *Château de Bizy.* Drive through Vernon and cross over to the other side of the Seine. Immediately beyond the bridge turn off for *Giverny (p. 49)*. Here you will find the estate which belonged to the great Impressionist, Claude Monet. It is one of Normandy's most beautiful attractions. Return to Vernon, stay on the right-hand side of the river and go along the D 313 to *Les Andelys (p. 49)* which is picturesquely situated in a loop of the Seine. At the end of the little town, the road leads up to the ruins of the *Château Gaillard.* Richard the Lionheart had the powerful stronghold built in 1196 to defend Normandy against the kingdom of the French. Driving on from here you can either go directly onto Rouen on the D 126 or you can take a scenic detour through the lovely countryside along the banks of the Seine. In *Amfreville* have a look at the unusual locks and enjoy the fantastic view of the Seine Valley from the *Côte des Deux Amants.* You should allow at least three hours to walk around the open-air "museum" of *Rouen (p. 39).* When you set off again, stay on the right-hand bank of the Seine and then, just before the beginning of the A 15, turn left onto the D 982. It is well worth making a stop in *St-Martin-de-Boscherville (p. 43)* to see the Norman Romanesque abbey church of *St-Georges.* The next place of interest is a real gem of religious architecture, the *Abbaye de Jumièges (p. 42),* considered to be the finest ruin in France. In *St-Wandrille-Rançon (p. 43)* you can visit the lovely 7th-century Benedictine abbey and, in *Caudebec-en-Caux (p. 42)*, visit the church of Notre-Dame, a masterpiece of Late Gothic architecture. Then leave the D 982 and take the D 81 to *Villquier*, a lovely town on the banks of the Seine, where you can pay homage to Victor Hugo. In a museum dedicated to the famous writer you can learn about the tragic circumstances of the death of his favourite daughter, Léopoldine. A few kilometres further on you come to the Late Gothic *Château d'Ételan*. In *Lillebonne* turn back along the D 982. The *Théâtre-amphithéâtre romain* which was built in the 1st century bears witness to the importance of the little town during the time of Julius Caesar. The A 131 goes directly to the major seaport of *Le Havre (p. 35)*, also known as *La Porte Océane*. The town suffered terrible destruction during World War II and has been rebuilt in a rather unimaginative fashion, offering few tourist attractions. Thus it is worth driving straight through to the suburb of *Ste-Adresse (p. 36)* . Make for the neo-Gothic chapel of *Notre-Dame-des-Flots* from where you can enjoy the view over the *Cap de la Hève*, the old *Fort de Ste-Adresse* and, of course, the sea.

② ALONG THE CÔTE D'ALBÂTRE

The exciting route to approach Normandy is from the north-east corner, from the seaside resort of *Le Tréport*. Lying picturesquely at the foot of the highest cliffs in France, Le Tréport reveals the great charm of the Côte d'Albâtre, which extends from here as far as Etretat. The coastline forms the edge of the chalk plateau of the Pays de Caux, delighting visitors with its extraordinarily dramatic rock formations. If you keep going across the Pont de Normandie, you will find the continuation of the coast in the lovely Côte Fleurie. The distance from Le Tréport to Etretat is 105 km and can easily be covered in half a day.

The steep cliffs tower up to a height of 100 metres in places. The green valleys are reached by the D 925, which snakes round countless bends along the edge of the cliffs to the *Cap de la Hève. Le Tréport (p. 34)* and the neighbouring bathing resort of *Mers-les-Bains* provide a lovely starting point for the coastal tour. It is well worth making a little excursion to the nearby town of *Eu (p. 34)*, with its château which is as magnificent as it is rich in history. Next you come to France's oldest seaside resort, *Dieppe (p. 32)*. The castle which towers above the town and the harbour emphasises the mediaeval character of Dieppe. The D 75 and D 68 take the next leg of the tour along the coast. It is worth making a stop in *Varengeville-sur-Mer (p. 35)*. The wonderful church which is situated above the sea in the artists' village has a fine stained glass window designed by Georges Braque. A few kilometres further on you will reach the next popular seaside resort of St-Valéry-en-Caux. The town's main attraction is the picturesque *Maison Henri-IV*, which is situated on the *Quai du Havre*. A detour inland takes you to *Cany Barville (p. 37)* to the Château de Cany, which enjoys a splendid location in the middle of a beautiful park. The D 925 now leads straight to *Fécamp,* which can also be reached by going along the coast road via *Veulettes-sur-Mer (p. 38).* This route also takes you past the *Château de Sassetot. Fécamp (p. 38)* is a town which is full of interesting facets to be discovered one after the other. The undisputed highlight is the immense Early Gothic abbey church of Sainte-Trinité. Just down the coast from Fécamp is Yport, a charming little bathing resort which nestles close to the steep cliffs. However, there is much more space on the beach at *Etretat (p. 37)* not to mention the two natural wonders on either side of it. These are the famous "needles" which have become one of the symbols of Normandy.

③ THROUGH THE QUIET HINTERLAND

The inland region is a landscape for quiet enjoyment. Anyone who knows the lovely route from Alençon through the Suisse Normande to the Calvados coastline will happily confirm this. On trips to the Normandy coast, you should not simply dive straight through the inland region without stopping. Instead, its magnificent architecture and beautiful countryside should be enjoyed at leisure. The route is around 140 km and takes about six hours.

Alençon (p. 83) has always been an important border town. Visitors are greeted here by the immense Château des Ducs and they soon become aware that they have entered a place rich in history. A few kilometres further on another attraction awaits you in the middle of the wonderful *Alpes Mancelles.* The picturesque village of *Saint-Céneri-le-Gérei (p. 87)* nestles in the hills and is one of France's 100 prettiest villages. After this little detour the route continues northwards along the N 138 to the diocesan town of *Sées (p. 87).* The imposing cathedral of Notre-Dame is a masterpiece of Norman High Gothic architecture. A few kilometres further along the N 158 brings you to a series of attractive châteaux, including the charming Château d'O in *Mortrée (p. 87),* the elegant Château de Sassy in *Saint-Christophe-le-Jajolet (p. 87)* and the château in *Médavy.* The D 26 leads to *Le Pin-au-Haras (p. 86)* to the stud farm which is also housed in a château, *Haras du Pin (p. 86).* The N 26 now takes you along a lovely scenic route to the town *Argentan (p. 85).* Like Alençon, this centre also owes its popular reputation to the famous tradition of lace-making. From here it is not far along the N 158 to *Falaise (p. 59),* the birthplace of the legendary Norman Duke, William the Conqueror. The D 511 takes you to the flower-bedecked *Pont-d'Ouilly (p. 95)* in the middle of the romantic *Suisse Normande.* Nature lovers and sports enthusiasts find plenty of opportunities to indulge in their hobbies to their heart's content in this extraordinarily beautiful, varied landscape. You can go walking, cycling, riding, rock-climbing, hang-gliding and, last but by no means least, canoeing and kayaking. The lively central focus of the region is the little town of *Clécy,* which tends to be very crowded. Relaxation and tranquillity can be found in the English park surrounding the ruined château in *Harcourt (p. 62).* Along the D 562 you finally reach the end of the route in *Caen (p. 57),* the former capital of Normandy. The magnificent buildings of the two famous abbeys and the fortifications are inextricably linked with the name of William the Conqueror.

④ EN ROUTE TO MONT SAINT MICHEL

The famous rock with its monastery in the Baie du Mont Saint Michel possesses an irresistible fascination of its own and no trip to Normandy is complete without a visit there. A pleasant route to the monastery starts in historic Bayeux, goes through richly varied landscapes passing châteaux and abbeys, includes some interesting towns and reaches its final destination at the "mystical sacred rock of the Western world". Day trip: 135 km

Bayeux (p. 53) boasts an enchanting place of interest in its splendid cathedral in the lovely Old Town. However, its greatest attraction is naturally the famous *Tapisserie de Bayeux,* which, in 70 metres of embroidered pictures, tells the story of the defeat of the English by the Norman Duke, William the Conqueror. Leave the town on the D 572 and drive as far as the *Forêt de Cerisy.* On the left-hand side is the exquisite *Château de Balleroy* where you can visit the hot-air ballooning museum. On the right-hand side is the romantic abbey church of *Cerisy-la-Forêt (p. 80).* Soon after this you will reach *St-Lô (p. 78).* The town's greatest treasure is the stud farm established by Napoléon Bonaparte, the *Haras National,* with over 100 valuable stallions. The cathedral of *Coutances (p. 80),* which is reached along the D 972, is a real architectural gem. It is an impressive example of the Norman Gothic style. From the terrace of the massive crossing tower the beaches of *Agon-Coutainville* can be seen. If visibility is good, it is even possible to see as far as the island of *Jersey.* If you have enough time, drive along the coast road. If not, the D 971 takes you straight to the town of *Granville (p. 71).* The popular seaside resort marks the beginning of the wide Baie du Mont Saint Michel and there is a wonderful panoramic view from the upper town. There is more than one way to get to Avranches: either go straight along the D 973 or take the coast road. It is well worth making a detour (28 km) to the mediaeval town of *Villedieu-les-Poêles (p. 72).* This is the town of the coppersmiths and bell-founders and it attracts large numbers of visitors. This is also true of the old diocesan town of *Avranches (p. 69),* where the *Jardin des Plantes* affords visitors a fantastic view of the sacred rock in the bay. After this it is only a few kilometres along the N 175 and the D 75 until you find yourself standing rapt in front of the legendary *Mont Saint Michel (p. 77).* The rocky island which is washed by the waves is linked to the mainland by a causeway so you can drive right up to the entrance to the monastery.

Practical information

The most important addresses and other information for your trip to Normandy

AMERICAN & BRITISH ENGLISH

Marco Polo travel guides are written in British English. In North America, certain terms and usages deviate from British usage. Some of the more frequently encountered examples are:
baggage for luggage, billion for thousand million, cab for taxi, car rental for car hire, drugstore for chemist's, fall for autumn, first floor for ground-floor, freeway/highway for motorway, gas(oline) for petrol, railroad for railway, restroom for toilet/lavatory, streetcar for tram, subway for underground/tube, toll-free numbers for freephone numbers, trailer for caravan, trunk for boot, vacation for holiday, wait staff for waiting staff (in restaurants etc.), zip code for postal code.

ANIMALS

Animals under three months old may not be brought into France. Although checks are not usually made, certificates of immunisation against hepatities and rabies should be taken.

BANKS

Bank opening hours are not standard. In the larger towns they are usually open *Mon–Fri 9 am– 4.30/5 pm.* In smaller towns banks are closed for lunch between *12.30 pm and 1.30/2 pm, open until 12 am on Sat* but closed all day on Mondays.

Service, charges and exchange rates also vary. Credit cards are increasingly widely accepted (especially Visa and Mastercard/ Eurocard). Eurocheques up to a value of 1,400 FF can be cashed.

BUSES AND TRAINS

France has an excellent rail network connecting all towns and cities. In rural areas the railway infrastructure is complemented by a well-developed bus network. Thus, the route to every town and village is quick, easy and safe. Timetables can be obtained from the *Office de Tourisme.*

CAMPING

Campers are always welcome in Normandy and accordingly there is a wide range of well-appointed campsites.

The categories range from fairly basic to luxury sites. In addition, there are *Aires naturelles de Camping* (small campsites in the open countryside) and *Camping à la Ferme* (farmhouses with basic facilities). Camping is only permitted at official sites.
Information: *Comité Régional du Tourisme de Normandie; 14, rue Charles Corbeau, 27000 Evreux; Tel. 0117 986 03 86.*

CUSTOMS

Goods for personal use can be imported from and exported to countries of the EU without restriction. Visitors from non-EU countries are allowed up to 200 cigarettes, 100 cigarillos, 50 cigars, 250 g of tobacco, 1 l of spirits more than 22%, 2 l wine and 50g of perfume and 250 ml of eau de toilette.

CYCLING TOURS

Normandy is the perfect setting for cycling tours. Bicycles can be rented from railway stations (look out for *train + vélo*), or you can choose to bring your own bike with you. The best way to plan your route is with Michelin Map No. 231 *Normandie*. Suggested routes are also available from the local *Offices de Tourisme* and from the *Fédération Française de Cyclotourisme; 8, rue Jean-Marie-Jego, 75013 Paris; Tel. 01 44 16 88 88.*

DOCTORS

In case of emergency, the police, *Tel. 17*, contact the ambulance or a doctor. Consultants charge between 120 and 150 FF and are to be paid in cash. It is recommended to take out medical insurance before travelling.

DRIVING

Speed limits are as follows: highways 130 (110 in rain) km/h, expressways 110 (100 in rain) km/h, national (N) and département roads (D) 90 (80 in rain) km/h and 50 km/h in built-up areas. The alcohol limit is 50 millilitres. Seatbelts must be worn. Motorbikes must drive with dipped headlights, as should all vehicles when it is foggy or raining.

People tend to drive fast in France, even in built-up areas. It is important not to be tempted to speed, as hefty fines are imposed, even in cases where the speed limit is only exceeded by a small amount. There are tolls on the highways – 100 km cost around 35 FF. The road network is well-maintained and plenty of signposts make navigation simple. There is usually a lot of traffic on the national (N) roads.

In case of accident, the police are only to be involved if someone is injured. Should you have a traffic accident, find two witnesses and inform your own insurer. Do not sign any admission of liability. In the event of minor accidents it is best to come to an agreement with the other party (usually under-insured). Travellers are advised to take out international travel cover as well as fully comprehensive insurance.

In case of breakdown, assistance is available from the police, *Tel. 17*, and from highway emergency phones.

Minor damage to vehicles can be repaired quickly, reliably and affordably at petrol station workshops. Lead-free petrol *(sans plomb)* is now available everywhere.

EMBASSIES

Embassies of the French Republic

4101 Reservoir Road, NW, Washington, DC 20007; Tel. (202) 944 60 00; Fax (202) 944 60 40; e-mail: info@amb-wash.fr

42 Sussex Drive, Ottawa, Ontario, K1M 2C9; Tel. (613) 789 17 95; Fax (613) 562 37 04; e-mail: consul@amba-ottawa.fr

58 Knightsbridge, London, SW1X 7JT; Tel. (020) 7201 1000 Fax (020) 7201 1059; e-mail: press@mail.ambafrance.org.uk

Embassy of the United States of America

2, avenue Gabriel, 75008 Paris, Cedex 08; Tel. (1) 43 12 22 22; Fax (1) 42 66 97 83

Canadian Embassy

35, avenue Montaigne, 75008 Paris; Tel. (1) 44 43 29 00; Fax (1) 44 43 25 12

British Embassy

35, rue de Faubourg St Honoré, 75383 Paris, Cedex 08; Tel. (1) 44 51 31 00; Fax (1) 44 51 32 88

EMERGENCIES

Police: *Police Secours; Tel. 17*
Fire: *Tel. 15*
Ambulance: *Tel. 15*

FISHING

In Normandy are plenty of opportunities for fishing, both on the coast and in inland rivers and

The beaches below the steep cliffs are the main attraction in summer

The Suisse Normande

One of the most beautiful parts of inland Normandy is the area known as Norman Switzerland. If you follow the signposted Route de la Suisse Normande, you will be taken through an unforgettable landscape of unique sights and impressions. The rivers and streams pass through rolling hills, picturesque valleys and steep rocky cliffs. Through the centre of the region, sometimes calm, sometimes turbulent, flows the Orne, carving its path deep into the rock. The route goes from Thury-Harcourt through Condé-sur-Noireau, Pont-d'Ouilly and Clécy and then back to Thury-Harcourt. It offers visitors a wealth of châteaux, churches, and charming villages and also provides a wide range of opportunities for walking and mountain biking. Riding, kite flying, climbing and canoeing and kayaking can also be enjoyed. *Detailed information is available from the Office de Tourisme; 14220 Thury-Harcourt, pl. St-Sauveur; Tel. 02 31 79 70 45.*

streams. Information about regulations for anglers is available from the *Fédération Départementale des Associations de Pêche et de Pisciculture.*

INFORMATION

Maison de la France
French Government Tourist Office

in the USA
16th Floor, 444 Madison Avenue, New York, NY 10022-6903; Tel. (212) 838 78 00; Fax (212) 838 78 55

in Canada
Suite 490, 1981 Avenue McGill College, Montréal, Québec H3A 2W9; Tel. (514) 288 42 64; Fax (514) 845 48 68; e-mail: mfrance@mtl.net

in the UK
178 Piccadilly, London, W1V 0AL; Tel. (0891) 244 123; Fax (020) 7493 6594; e-mail: info@mdl.co.uk

Information is available from the regional Offices de Tourisme and, in addition from the:
Comité Régional du Tourisme Normandie; 14 rue Charles Corbeau, 27000 Evreux; Tel. 0117 986 03 86; Fax 0117 986 03 79

MEASURES & WEIGHTS

1 cm	0.39 inches
1 m	1.09 yards (3.28 feet)
1 km	0.62 miles
1 m²	1.20 sq. yards
1 ha	2.47 acres
1 km²	0.39 sq. miles
1 g	0.035 ounces
1 kg	2.21 pounds
1 British tonne	1016 kg
1 US ton	907 kg

1 litre is equivalent to 0.22 Imperial gallons and 0.26 US

NEWSPAPERS

A wide range of French and international newpapers and magazines are available from the *maison de presse*, stationery shops, bookshops and tobacconists. Maybe you'll even find your favorite one!

NUDIST BATHING

No objections are raised against naturists in Normandy. In fact, on the contrary, the French hold *naturisme* in high regard. There are plenty of nice spots for naturists all along the coast, on sheltered beaches which are off the beaten track. Addresses and descriptions can be found in the naturists' guide, *Guide Naturiste Français; Socnat, 16, rue Drouot, 75009 Paris.*

OPENING HOURS

Fresh *baguettes* can be bought from bakeries mostly from 7 am.

Shops selling general groceries open at around 8 am, department stores and boutiques from 10 am at the latest. Except for supermarkets, most shops usually close for lunch from noon until 2 pm. Shops

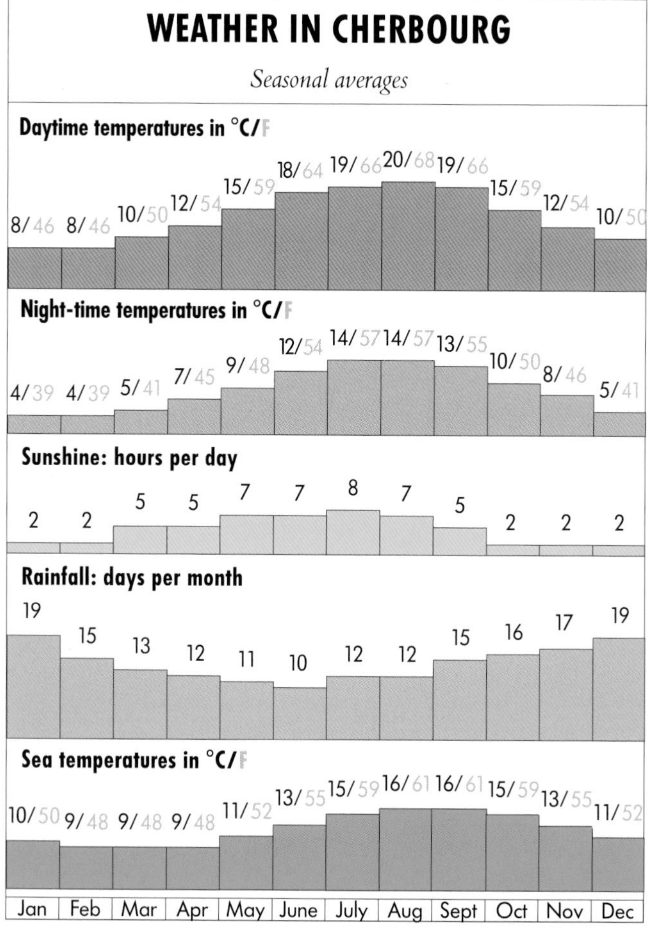

The River Orne from the Pont d'Ouilly

generally close 7/7.30 pm. Bakeries and shopping centres are also open on Sunday mornings. Most shops are closed all day on Mondays.

PASSPORT & VISA

Travellers require a valid passport or identity card.

POST & TELEPHONE

The post offices *(Poste* or *PTT)* are open *Mon–Fri 9 am–12 am and 2 pm–5 pm, Sat 9 am–12 am.*

International calls can be made from post offices or phone boxes. In most phone boxes you will require a *télécarte.* Phone cards are available from post offices, tobacconists, petrol stations and hotels. Phoning from France:

Dial 00, wait for the tone, then dial the country code: *UK: 44; USA and Canada: 1*

Then dial the area code without the "0" at the beginning followed by the number.

Phoning France:

Country code for France: 0033, then the area code withouth the "0" at the beginning.

TIPPING

A two franc coin is the lowest tip you should leave. Anything less than this is insulting. In hotels, whether it's for calling a taxi of for carrying your luggage, 10 FF is an appopriate tip. Chamber-maids expect around 10–20 FF. In restaurants, at the hairdressers and in taxis it is advisable to give a ten per cent tip.

VOLTAGE

220 V. French sockets take two-pin plugs so travellers are advised to bring an adapter.

YOUTH HOSTELS

Normandy boasts a range of youth hostels. With an international membership card you can stay in any of the hostels.

Do's and don'ts

How to avoid some of the traps and pitfalls that face the unwary traveller

Accommodation shortage
In July and August the whole of France goes *en vacance*. The number of people who want to spend their holidays on the sunny coast of Normandy is enormous. So it is no surprise that accommodation in the coastal resorts is quickly snapped up. People travelling at this time are advised to book hotel rooms, holiday cottages, apartments and even campsites well in advance. Anyone travelling before or after this period will have no problem finding accommodation. It's cheaper then too.

Danger at high tide
Every six hours, at low tide, the sea goes out a long way. When it turns and comes in again, it does so very quickly. In order to ensure that a quiet stroll along the beach doesn't turn into a panic-stricken sprint, it is advisable to check the times of high tide. Locals who are familiar with the sea, or the tourist office, can help with tide tables.

Fun in the waves
Before jumping straight into the waves, it is advisable to get used to the sea first. This is particularly important if you decide to swim in a quiet, unsupervised spot. If you have chosen a beach with lots of rocks, the incoming waves, strong currents and sudden changes in depth can be very dangerous, even for experienced swimmers. This is naturally also true if you are windsurfing or sailing: powerful waves and strong winds can appear out of nowhere, making it extremely difficult to control the surfboard or boat. So before frolicking in the foaming waves it is wise to check with a lifeguard or ask at a member of staff at the tourist office to show you which sections of the coast are safe.

Thieves
Anywhere where there are lots of people, there are also always lots of opportunities for thieves. It's the same everywhere. Cars are a prime target, especially when they are parked in a remote spot. You can at least minimise the risk by making sure your car is locked and that no valuable objects can be seen lying about inside. Don't forget, there are swarms of accomplished thieves, even in France.

A question of style
Don't forget that the clothes you would happily wear in your own garden are not necessarily appropriate for going to visit a venerable cathedral.

Road Atlas of Normandy

Please refer to back cover for an overview of this Road Atlas

A
B
C
1
2
3
4
5
6
10 km
Guernsey
Alderney
St. Anne
Pointe Quénard
Cap de la
Goury
Jobourg
Nez de Voidries
Nez de Jobourg
Herqueville
Vauville
Weymouth 2½h
Poole 2h
Poole 8h
Portsmouth 9h
Vale
Copo Bay
St. Sampson
L'Etacq
Jethou
Herm
St. Peter-Port
St. Martin
Icart Point
Sark
Diélette
Cap de Flamanville
Flamanville
Pointe du Rozel
Surtainville
Carteret
Cap de Carteret
Passage de la Déroute
Channel Islands
GREAT BRITAIN
Plymouth 8h
Grottes Plémont
Mailresse Ile
St. John
Trinity
St.Ouen's Bay
St. Peter
Jersey
Zoo
St. Martin
St. Brelade
Hougue-Bie
Mont Orgueil
St. Aubin
Gorey
ST. HELIER
St. Clément
la Rocque Pointe
Golfe de St. Malo
Iles Chausey
Grande Ile
Granvi
Pointe du Roc
Baie de St. Brieuc
Côte d'Emeraude
Cap Fréhel
Sables d'Or-les Pins
Fort de la Latte
Erquy
Fréhel
St. Cast
Pointe de St. Cast
Pointe du Grouin
Baie du Mont St. Michel
Pointe de la Chaine
Cancale
Pléneuf-Val-André
Guildo
Pen Guen Plage
Pointe du Chevet
St. Lunaire
Rothéneuf
PARAMÉ
ST. MALO
Dinard
St. Alban
Hénanbihen
Matignon
St. Jacut-de-la-Mer
St. Briac-s.-Mer
St. Méloir-des-Ondes
St. Gueltas
le Guildo
Ploubalay
Usine Marem.
la Gouesnière
Cherrueix
St. Suliac
le Vivier-s.-Mer
Mont Dol
Plancoët
Pleslin
Pléven
Lamballe
Plédéliac
Bourseul
Languen
Châteauneuf-d'Ille-et-Vilaine
Pleudihen-
Dol-
St. Broladre
Cout
Pointe
106
100

D
E
F
1
2
3
4
5
Portsmouth 5-9h
Southamton 5h
Poole 3½h
Querqueville
Cap Lévy
Fermanville
Gatteville-le-Phare
Pointe de Barfleur
Barfleur
St. Pierre-Eglise
Tourlaville
la Glacerie
le Vast
Martinvast
le Theil
la Pernelle
Pointe de Saire
Ile de Tatihou
Quettehou
St. Vaast-la-Hougue
Délasse
Valognes
Quinéville
Bricquebec
Montebourg
les Gougins
Baie de
Colomby
Orglandes
Ravenoville
St. Sauveur-le-Vicomte
Utah Beach
Ste. Mère-Eglise
la Madeleine
Pont l'Abbé
Chef-du-Pont
Ste. Marie-du-Mont
Grandcamp-les-Bains
Pointe du Hoc
Vierville-s.-Mer
Côte
St. Côme-du-Mont
St. Pierre-du-Mont
Omaha Beach
Colleville-s.-Mer
Port-en-Bessin
la Haye-du-Puits
Baupte
Osmanville
la Cambe
Mont Castre
St. Jores
Carentan
Isigny-sur-Mer
Formigny
Trévières
St. Germain-sur-Ay
Catz
Arromanches-les-Bains
Lessay
St. Patrice-de-Claids
Colombières
Mosles
Tour-en-Bessin
Sainteny
St. Jean-de-Daye
Airel
Bayeux
Périers
Tribehou
le Molay-Littry
la Mine
les Camps-de-Losque
Cerisy-la-Forêt
Martragny
St. Sauveur-Lendelin
le Mesnil-Vigot
Juaye-Mondaye
St. Clair-s.-l'Elle
Balleroy
Pont-Hébert
Forêt de Cerisy
Abb. de Mondaye
Montsurvent
Tilly-s.-Seulles
Gratot
Marigny
Agneaux
St. Lô
Juvigny-s.-Seulles
Coutances
Canisy
St. Jean-des-Baisants
Caumont-l'Eventé
Tourville-s.-Sienne
St. Samson-de-Bonfossé
Cerisy-la-Salle
Dangy
Condé-sur-Vire
Torigni-sur-Vire
Seulles
Villers-Bocage
Notre-Dame-de-Cenilly
le Mesnil-Herman
Roches de Ham
les Montagnes
Coulvain
Quettreville
Aunay-sur-Odon
Villebaudon
Tessy-s.-Vire
St. Martin-des-Besaces
Jurques
Lengronne
Hambye
Mont Robin
Bréhal
Cérences
Anc. Abb. d'Hambye
Pont-Farcy
le Bény-Bocage
Montamy
Mont Pinçon
Ver
Gavray
Percy
Danvou-la-Ferrière
Montaigu-les-Bois
Beaumesnil
la Graverie
St. Pierre-la-Vieille
Beauchamps
Villedieu-les-Poêles
Estry
St. Sever-Calvados
Pontécoulant
la Haye-Pesnel
Vire
Vassy
Sartilly
Sienne
St. Germain-du-Crioult
St. Laurent-de-Cuves
Truttemer
Athis-de-l'Orne
Gathemo
Genêts
Ponts
Brécey
St. Pois
Tinchebray
Avranches
Chérencé-le-Roussel
Sourdeval
St. Cornier-des-Landes
Flers
St. Quentin-s.-le-Homme
Pontaubault
Reffuveille
Juvigny-le-Tertre
Ger
Ducey
Mortain
la Ferrière-aux-Etangs
Isigny-le-Buat
Lonlay-l'Abbaye
107

A
B
C
Portsmouth 5-6h
Pointe de Barfleur
Barfleur
Gatteville-le-Phare
Pointe de Saire
Ile de Tatihou
St. Vaast-la-Hougue
Quinéville
les Gougins
Baie de la Se
Ravenoville
Utah Beach
Ste. Mère-Eglise
la Madeleine
Ste. Marie-du-Mont
Grandcamp-les-Bains
Pointe du Hoc
Côte de Nacre
Vierville-s.-Mer
Omaha Beach
St. Pierre-du-Mont
Colleville-s.-Mer
Port-en-Bessin
St. Côme-du-Mont
Osmanville
la Cambe
Isigny-sur-Mer
Formigny
Trévières
Colombières
Mosles
Tour-en-Bessin
Arromanches-les-Bains
Gold Beach
Courseulles-sur-Mer
St. Aubin-s.-Mer
Vers-s.-Mer
Juno Beach
Langrune
Crépon
Bayeux
Creully
Brécy
Douvres-la-Délivrande
Luc-sur-Mer
St. Jean-de-Daye
Airel
le Molay-Littry
la Mine
Cerisy-la-Forêt
Forêt de Cerisy
Juaye-Mondaye
Martragny
Anc. Eglise de Thaon
Fontaine-Henry
Thaon
Mathieu
Riva-Bella
Ouistreham
Bénouville
les Champs-de-Losque
St. Clair-s.-l'Elle
Balleroy
Abb. de Mondaye
Bretteville-l'Orgueilleuse
HÉROUVILLE ST. CLAIR
Pont-Hébert
Agneaux
St. Lô
Tilly-s.-Seulles
Carpiquet
St. Jean-des-Baisants
Caumont-l'Evente
Juvigny-s.-Seulles
St.-Martin
Bretteville-s.-Odon
CA
St. Samson-de-Bonfossé
Condé-sur-Vire
Dangy
Torigni-sur-Vire
Fleury-s.-Orne
Ifs
Villers-Bocage
Evrecy
le Mesnil-Herman
Roches de Ham
les Montagnes
Coulvain
Amaye-s.-Orne
Laize-la-Ville
Tessy-s.-Vire
St. Martin-des-Besaces
Jurques
Aunay-sur-Odon
les Moutiers-en-Cinglais
Bretteville-s.-Laize
Percy
Pont-Farcy
le Bény-Bocage
Collines
Montamy
Mont Pinçon
Barbery
Thury-Harcourt
Danvou-la-Ferrière
le Plessis-Grimoult
Caumont-s.-Orne
Beaumesnil
la Graverie
St. Pierre-la-Vieille
Mont de Pêre
St. Clair
Ussy
Estry
Clécy
St. Sever-Calvados
Pontécoulant
La Suisse Normande
Vire
Vassy
St. Germain-du-Crioult
Condé-sur-Noireau
Pont-d'Ouilly
St. Laurent-de-Cuves
Truttemer
St. Pois
Gathemo
Athis-de-L'Orne
Roche d'Oëtre
Ménil-Hermei
Taillebois
Bazoches-au-Hou
Tinchebray
Sourdeval
St. Georges-des-Groseilliers
Ste. Honorine-la-Guillaume
Chérencé-le-Roussel
St. Cornier-des-Landes
Flers
Landigou
Reffuveille
Juvigny-le-Tertre
Ger
Messei
Putanges
Fromentel
Beauchêne
Briouze
St. Hilaire-
107
102

D
E
F
Côte d'Alb
Veulettes-sur-Mer
St. Valery-en-Caux
St. Pierre-en-Port
Sassetot-le-Mauconduit
Eletot
N.-D.-du-Salut
Fécamp
Yport
Valleuse du Curé
Étretat
Falaise d'Aval
Cap d'Antifer
Benouville
les Loges
Toussaint
Valmont
Cany-Barville
Ourville-en-Caux
Auffay
Angerville-Bailleul
Criquetot-l.-Esneval
Bruneval
Gonneville-la-Mallet
Goderville
Fauville-en-Caux
Hericourt-en-Caux
Pays de Caux
Rouville
Octeville-sur-Mer
Épouville
Beuzeville-la-Grenier
Alliquerville
Yvetot
Montivilliers
St. Rom.-de-C.
Bolbec
Harfleur
Ste. Adresse
Le Havre
Gonfreville l'Or
Route Ind.
St. Romain-de-Colbosc
Tancarville
Lillebonne
Caudebec-en-Caux
N.-D.-de-Gravenchon
Pont de Normandie
Seine
Pont de Tancarville
Berville-s.-Mer
Honfleur
Quillebeuf-sur-Seine
Norville
St. Maurice-d'Etelan
Maillerave-sur-Seine
Pointe de la Roque
Villerville
Côte Fleurie
Trouville-sur-Mer
Fiquefleur
Barneville
Foulbec
St. Samson-de-Roque
Jumièges
la Haye-de Routot
Deauville
Blonville-s.-Mer
Falaises des Vaches Noires
Canisy
St. Maclou
Bourneville
Beuzeville
Villers-s.-Mer
St. André d'Hébertot
Tancarville
Bourg-Achard
Houlgate
Dives-sur-Mer
Beaumont-en-Auge
Pont-l'Évêque
Pont-Audemer
Corneville-s.-Risle
Appeville-Annebault
Annebault
Epaignes
Campigny
Autoroute de Normandie
Dozulé
Valsemé
Blangy-le-Chât.
Cormeilles
St. Georges-du-Vièvre
Boissey-le-Châtel
Beuvron-en-Auge
le Breuil-en-Auge
Lieurey
Le Neubourg
Manerbe
Moyan
Calonne
le Bec Hellouin
la Boissière
Quilly-du-Houley
Brionne
Bazoques
Harcourt
Mèzidon-Canon
Crèvecœur-en-Auge
Lisieux
Thiberville
la Rivière-Thibouville
Chât. du Champ-de-Bataille
Vieux-Fumé
St. Julien-le-Faucon
St. Martin-de-la-Lieue
St. Germain-de-Livet
Bernay
Serquigny
Pays d'Auge
Boissey
Fervaques
Beaumont-le-Roger
St. Pierre-sur-Dives
Livarot
Orbec
Emanville
Jort
Broglie
Beaumesnil
Bellou
Landepereuse
Ammeville
Meulles
Vimoutiers
Courteilles
la Barre-en-Ouche
la Ferrière-s.-Risle
Camembert
Montreuil-l'Argillé
St. Pierre-du-Mesnil
Pays d'Ouche
Trun
le Sap
Monnai
la Vieille-Lyre
Villers-en-Ouche
Glos-la-Ferrière
les Baux-de-Breteuil
Chambois
St. Nicolas-des-Laitiers
la Ferté-Frênel
le Bourg-St. Léonard
Dives
Gacé
Rugles
Breteuil
Argentan
Exmes
Haras du Pin
St. Evroult-N.-D.-du-Bois
l'Aigle
Echauffour
Touques
Vie
Risle
Charentonne
Orne
103
108
10 km

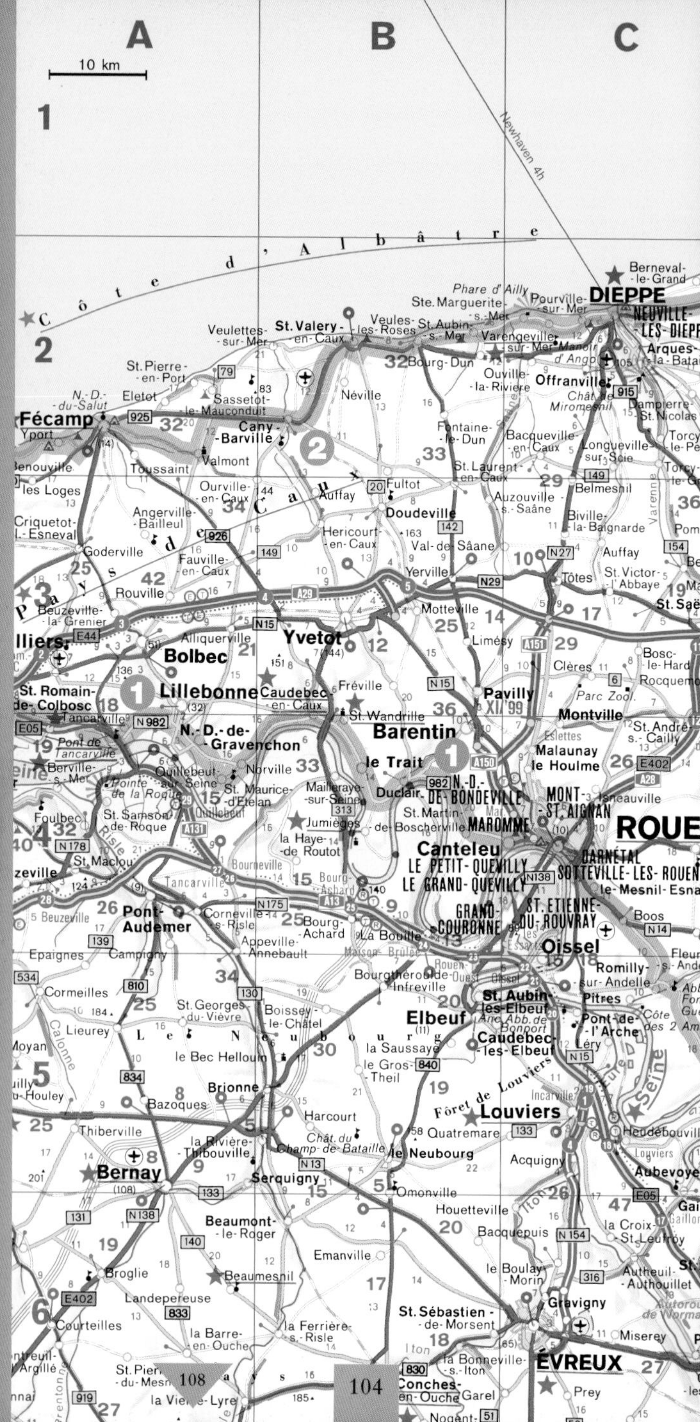
A
B
C
10 km
1
2
Newhaven 4h
Côte d'Albâtre
Berneval-le-Grand
Phare d'Ailly
Ste. Marguerite
Pourville-sur-Mer
DIEPPE
NEUVILLE-LES-DIEPPE
Veulettes-sur-Mer
St. Valery-en-Caux
Veules-les-Roses
St. Aubin-s.-Mer
Varengeville-sur-Mer
Manoir d'Ango
Arques-la-Bataille
St. Pierre-en-Port
Sassetot-le-Mauconduit
Bourg-Dun
Ouville-la-Rivière
Offranville
N.-D.-du-Salut
Eletot
Néville
Château de Miromesnil
Dampierre-St. Nicolas
Fécamp
Yport
Cany-Barville
Fontaine-le-Dun
Bacqueville-en-Caux
Longueville-sur-Scie
Torcy-le-Petit
Benouville
Toussaint
Valmont
St. Laurent-en-Caux
Torcy-le-Grand
les Loges
Ourville-en-Caux
Auffay
Fultot
Belmesnil
Doudeville
Auzouville-s.-Saâne
Pays de Caux
Angerville-Bailleul
Criquetot-l'Esneval
Hericourt-en-Caux
Biville-la-Baignarde
Varenne
Goderville
Val-de-Sâane
Auffay
Fauville-en-Caux
Yerville
Tôtes
St. Victor-l'Abbaye
Rouville
Beuzeville-la-Grenier
Motteville
St. Saëns
Alliquerville
Yvetot
Limésy
Bolbec
Clères
Bosc-le-Hard
Rocquemont
St. Romain-de-Colbosc
Lillebonne
Caudebec-en-Caux
Fréville
Pavilly
Parc Zool.
Tancarville
St. Wandrille
Montville
N.-D.-de-Gravenchon
Barentin
St. André-s.-Cailly
Pont de Tancarville
Eslettes
Malaunay
le Houlme
Berville-s.-Mer
Quillebeuf-sur-Seine
Norville
le Trait
Seine
Pointe de la Roque
St. Maurice-d'Etelan
Mailleraye-sur-Seine
Duclair
N.-D.-DE-BONDEVILLE
MONT-ST. AIGNAN
Isneauville
Foulbec
St. Samson-de-Roque
Jumièges
St. Martin-de-Boscherville
MAROMME
ROUEN
la Haye-de Routot
Canteleu
DARNÉTAL
St. Maclou
Bourneville
LE PETIT-QUEVILLY
SOTTEVILLE-LES-ROUEN
Tancarville
Bourg-Achard
LE GRAND-QUEVILLY
le Mesnil-Esnard
Pont-Audemer
Corneville-s.-Risle
GRAND-COURONNE
ST. ETIENNE-DU-ROUVRAY
Boos
Beuzeville
Bourg-Achard
la Bouille
Oissel
Appeville-Annebault
Maison Brûlée
Epaignes
Campigny
Rouen-Ouest
Romilly-sur-Andelle
Bourgtheroulde-Infreville
Cormeilles
St. Georges-du-Vièvre
Boissey-le-Châtel
St. Aubin-lès-Elbeuf
Pitres
Elbeuf
Anc. Abb. de Bonport
Pont-de-l'Arche
Côte des 2 Amants
Lieurey
Le Neubourg
Calonne
Caudebec-lès-Elbeuf
Moyan
la Saussaye
Léry
le Bec Hellouin
le Gros-Theil
Forêt de Louviers
Brionne
Incarville
Bazoques
Louviers
Harcourt
Thiberville
Quatremare
Heudebouville
la Rivière-Thibouville
Chât. du Champ-de-Bataille
le Neubourg
Acquigny
Bernay
Serquigny
Aubevoye
Omonville
Houetteville
Beaumont-le-Roger
Gaillon
Bacquepuis
la Croix-St. Leufroy
Emanville
Broglie
le Boulay-Morin
Autheuil-Authouillet
Beaumesnil
Landepereuse
Gravigny
St. Sébastien-de-Morsent
Courteilles
la Barre-en-Ouche
la Ferrière-s.-Risle
Miserey
la Bonneville-s.-Iton
ÉVREUX
St. Pierre-du-Mesnil
Conches-en-Ouche
Garel
Prey
la Vieille-Lyre
Nogent-le-Sec
Iton
Risle
Eure

108

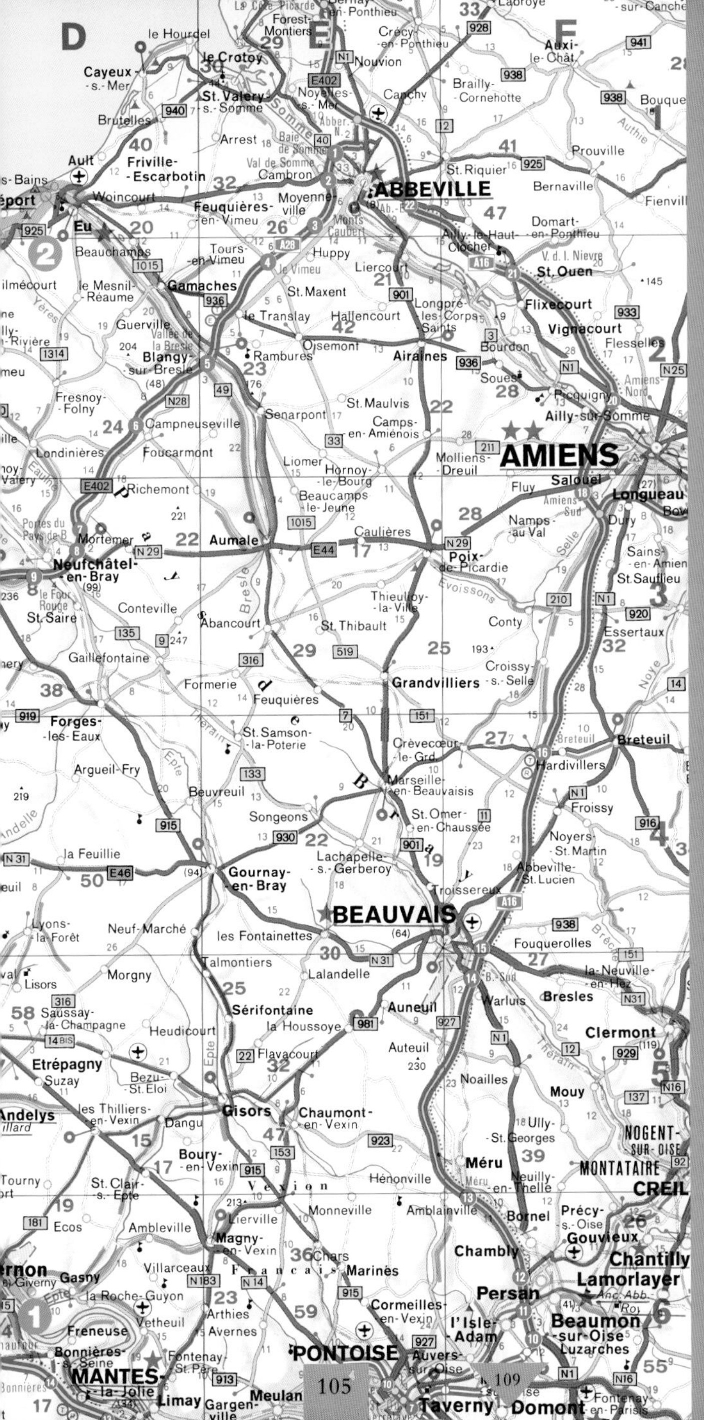

D
E
F
le Hourdel
le Crotoy
Cayeux-s.-Mer
St. Valery-s.-Somme
Brutelles
Forest-Montiers
Crécy-en-Ponthieu
Nouvion
Noyelles-s.-Mer
Canchy
Brailly-Cornehotte
Auxi-le-Chât.
Bouque
Arrest
Baie de Somme
Val de Somme
Cambron
Ault
Friville-Escarbotin
Woincourt
Eu
Beauchamps
Feuquières-en-Vimeu
Moyenneville
ABBEVILLE
Monts Caubert
St. Riquier
Bernaville
Prouville
Fienvill
Domart-en-Ponthieu
Ailly-le-Haut-Clocher
V. d. l. Nievre
St. Ouen
Tours-en-Vimeu
Huppy
le Vimeu
Liercourt
Gamaches
le Mesnil-Réaume
St. Maxent
Longpré-les-Corps-Saints
Flixecourt
Vignacourt
Flesselles
le Translay
Hallencourt
Oisemont
Airaines
Bourdon
Guerville
Vallée de la Bresle
Blangy-sur-Bresle
Rambures
Soues
Picquigny
Ailly-sur-Somme
Amiens-Nord
Fresnoy-Folny
Senarpont
St. Maulvis
Camps-en-Amiénois
Campneuseville
Foucarmont
Londinières
Liomer
Hornoy-le-Bourg
Molliens-Dreuil
AMIENS
Salouel
Fluy
Amiens Sud
Longueau
Richemont
Beaucamps-le-Jeune
Namps-au-Val
Dury
Portes du Pays de B.
Mortemer
Aumale
Caulières
Poix-de-Picardie
Sains-en-Amien
Neufchâtel-en-Bray
le Four Rouge
St. Saire
Conteville
Abancourt
Thieuloy-la-Ville
Evoissons
St. Saufflieu
Conty
Essertaux
St. Thibault
Gaillefontaine
Croissy-s.-Selle
Formerie
Feuquières
Grandvilliers
Forges-les-Eaux
St. Samson-la-Poterie
Crèvecœur-le-Grd.
Breteuil
Hardivillers
Argueil-Fry
Beuvreuil
Marseille-en-Beauvaisis
Froissy
Songeons
St. Omer-en-Chaussée
Noyers-St. Martin
la Feuillie
Gournay-en-Bray
Lachapelle-s.-Gerberoy
Abbeville-St. Lucien
Troissereux
BEAUVAIS
Lyons-la-Forêt
Neuf-Marché
les Fontainettes
Fouquerolles
Talmontiers
Lalandelle
la-Neuville-en-Hez
Lisors
Morgny
Warluis
Bresles
Saussay-la-Champagne
Sérifontaine
Auneuil
Heudicourt
la Houssoye
Clermont
Etrépagny
Flavacourt
Auteuil
Suzay
Bezu-St. Eloi
Noailles
Mouy
Andelys
les Thilliers-en-Vexin
Gisors
Chaumont-en-Vexin
Dangu
Ully-St. Georges
NOGENT-SUR-OISE
Boury-en-Vexin
Méru
MONTATAIRE
Tourny
St. Clair-s.-Epte
Vexion
Hénonville
Neuilly-en-Thelle
CREIL
Ecos
Ambleville
Lierville
Monneville
Amblainville
Bornel
Précy-s.-Oise
Gouvieux
Magny-en-Vexin
Chars
Chambly
Chantilly
Vernon
Giverny
Gasny
Villarceaux
Français
Marines
Lamorlayer
La Roche-Guyon
Persan
Anc. Abb.
Arthies
Cormeilles-en-Vexin
Freneuse
Vetheuil
Avernes
l'Isle-Adam
Beaumont-sur-Oise
Luzarches
Bonnières-s.-Seine
Fontenay-St. Père
PONTOISE
Auvers-sur-Oise
MANTES-la-Jolie
Limay
Gargenville
Meulan
Taverny
Domont
Fontenay-en-Parisis
Somme
Authie
Bresle
Selle
Noye
Epte
Thérain
Brêche
A28
A16
E402
E44
E46
N1
N29
N31
105
109

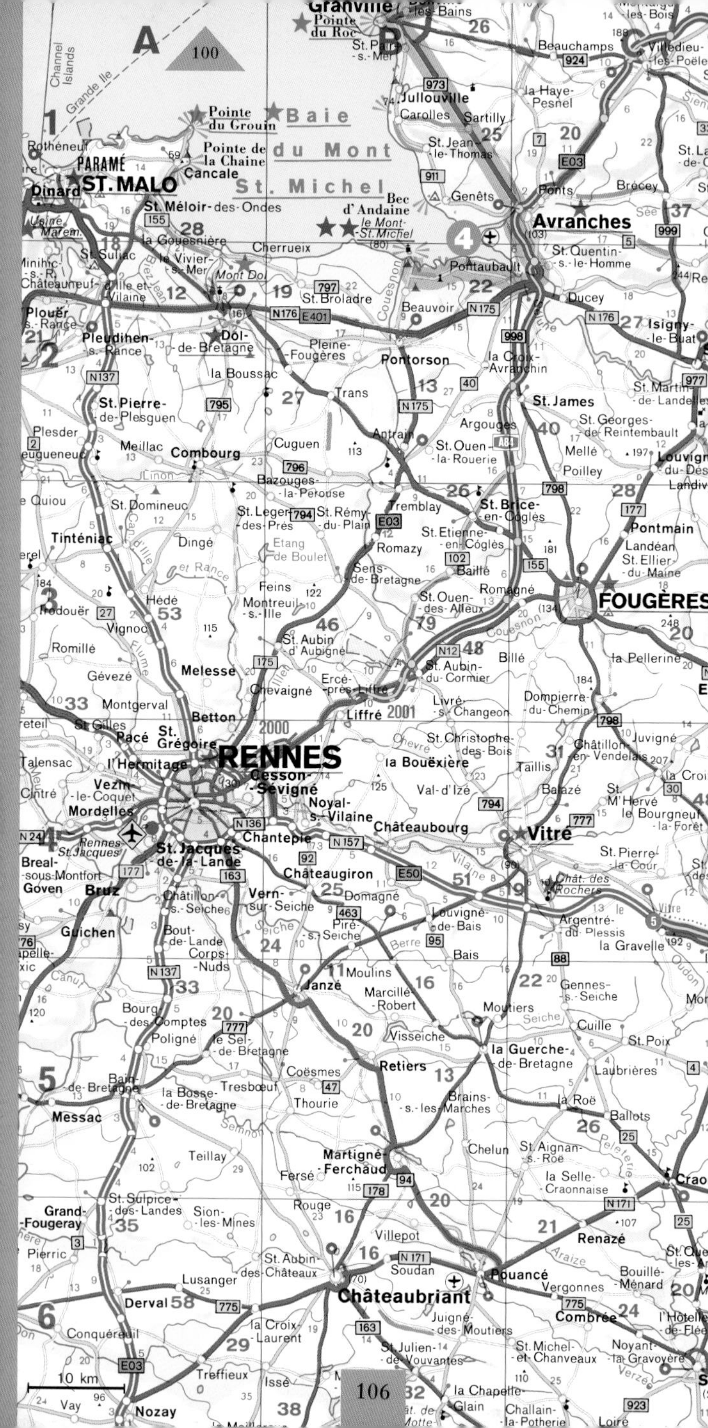
Granville
Pointe du Roc
St. Pair-s.-Mer
Jullouville
Carolles
Sartilly
St. Jean-le-Thomas
Genêts
Avranches
Villedieu-les-Poêles
Beauchamps
la Haye-Pesnel
Brécey
Pontaubault
Ducey
Isigny-le-Buat
St. Quentin-s.-le-Homme
Pointe du Grouin
Pointe de la Chaine
Cancale
Baie du Mont St. Michel
Bec d'Andaine
le Mont-St. Michel
Channel Islands
Grande Ile
Rothéneuf
PARAMÉ
ST. MALO
Dinard
St. Méloir-des-Ondes
la Gouesnière
Cherrueix
St. Suliac
le Vivier-s.-Mer
Mont Dol
Châteauneuf-d'Ille-et-Vilaine
St. Broladre
Beauvoir
Plouër-s.-Rance
Pleudihen-s.-Rance
Dol-de-Bretagne
Pleine-Fougères
Pontorson
la Croix-Avranchin
St. James
la Boussac
Trans
St. Pierre-de-Plesguen
Plesder
Meillac
Combourg
Cuguen
Antrain
St. Ouen-la-Rouerie
Argouges
St. Georges-de-Reintembault
Mellé
Poilley
Louvigné-du-Désert
Landivy
Bazouges-la-Perouse
Tremblay
St. Brice-en-Coglès
Pontmain
Landéan
St. Ellier-du-Maine
St. Domineuc
St. Leger-des-Prés
St. Rémy-du-Plain
St. Etienne-en-Coglès
Tinténiac
Dingé
Etang de Boulet
Romazy
Baillé
Sens-de-Bretagne
Romagné
FOUGÈRES
Feins
Montreuil-s.-Ille
St. Ouen-des-Alleux
Hédé
Irodouër
Vignoc
St. Aubin-d'Aubigné
Romillé
Gévezé
Melesse
Billé
St. Aubin-du-Cormier
la Pellerine
Ercé-près-Liffré
Chevaigné
Montgerval
Betton
Liffré
Livré-s.-Changeon
Dompierre-du-Chemin
St. Gilles
Pacé
St. Grégoire
RENNES
Cesson-Sévigné
St. Christophe-des-Bois
Châtillon-en-Vendelais
Juvigné
Talensac
l'Hermitage
la Bouëxière
Taillis
Vezin-le-Coquet
Cintré
Mordelles
Noyal-s.-Vilaine
Val-d'Izé
Balazé
St. M'Hervé
le Bourgneuf-la-Forêt
Chantepie
Châteaubourg
Vitré
Breal-sous-Montfort
Goven
Bruz
St. Jacques-de-la-Lande
Rennes-St. Jacques
Châteaugiron
St. Pierre-la-Cour
Chât. des Rochers
Châtillon-s.-Seiche
Vern-sur-Seiche
Domagné
Guichen
Bout-de-Lande
Corps-Nuds
Piré-s.-Seiche
Louvigné-de-Bais
Argentré-du-Plessis
la Gravelle
Bais
Moulins
Janzé
Marcillé-Robert
Gennes-s.-Seiche
Bourg-des-Comptes
Poligné
le Sel-de-Bretagne
Moutiers
Cuillé
Visseiche
St. Poix
la Guerche-de-Bretagne
Retiers
Coësmes
Laubrières
Bain-de-Bretagne
Messac
la Bosse-de-Bretagne
Tresbœuf
Thourie
Brains-s.-les-Marches
la Roë
Ballots
Teillay
Martigné-Ferchaud
Chelun
St. Aignan-s.-Roë
Fersé
la Selle-Craonnaise
Craon
St. Sulpice-des-Landes
Grand-Fougeray
Sion-les-Mines
Rouge
Renazé
Pierric
Villepot
St. Aubin-des-Châteaux
Soudan
Pouancé
Bouillé-Ménard
Lusanger
Derval
Châteaubriant
Vergonnes
Combrée
l'Hôtellerie-de-Flée
Conquéreuil
la Croix-Laurent
Juigné-des-Moutiers
St. Julien-de-Vouvantes
St. Michel-et-Chanveaux
Noyant-la-Gravoyère
Treffieux
Issé
la Chapelle-Glain
Challain-la-Potherie
Vay
Nozay
10 km
Linon
Couesnon
Vilaine
Seiche
Semnon
Araize
Verzée
Oudon
Chevré
Ille
Flume
Canut
Berre
Sélune
Sée
N176
N175
N137
N136
N157
N12
N171
E401
E03
E50
A84
2000
2001
100
A
B
C
1
2
3
4
5
6

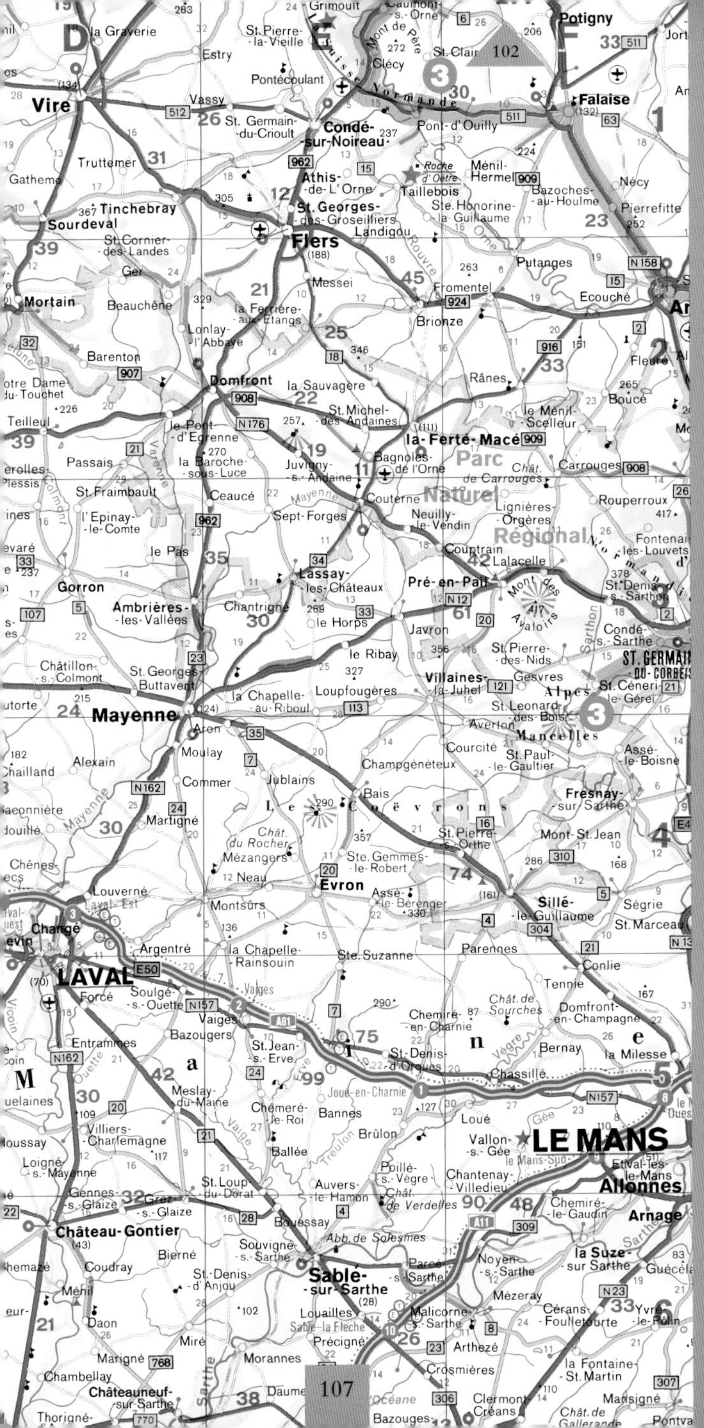

Vire
Flers
Condé-sur-Noireau
Falaise
Tinchebray
Sourdeval
Mortain
Domfront
la Ferté-Macé
Bagnoles-de l'Orne
Parc Naturel Régional Normandie
Lassay-les-Châteaux
Pré-en-Pail
Gorron
Ambrières-les-Vallées
Mayenne
Villaines-la-Juhel
Alpes Mancelles
Evron
Sillé-le-Guillaume
Fresnay-sur-Sarthe
Les Coëvrons
LAVAL
Château-Gontier
Sablé-sur-Sarthe
LE MANS
Allonnes
Arnage
la Suze-sur Sarthe
Meslay-du-Maine
Ste. Suzanne
Châteauneuf-sur-Sarthe
107
102

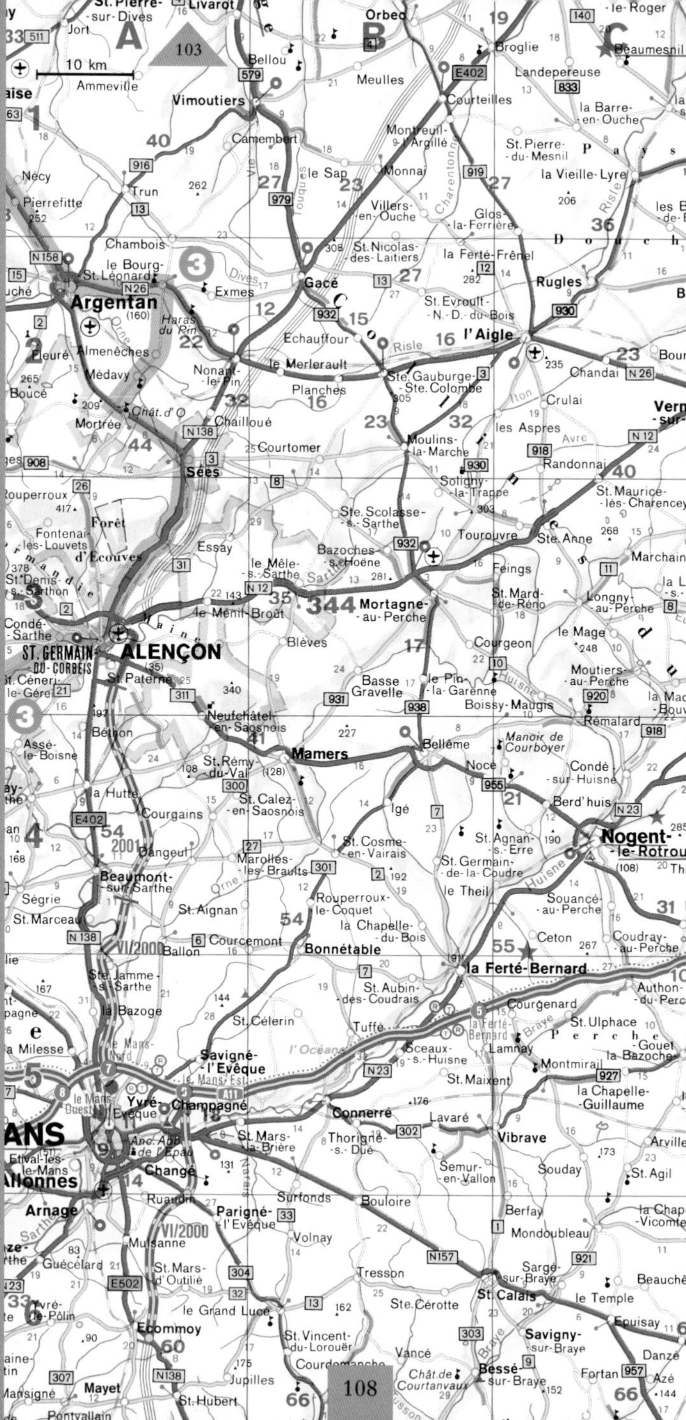

St. Pierre-sur-Dives
Livarot
Orbec
-le-Roger
Jort
A
103
B
C
Broglie
Beaumesnil
10 km
Ammeville
Bellou
Meulles
Landepereuse
Vimoutiers
Courteilles
la Barre-en-Ouche
Camembert
Montreuil-l'Argillé
St. Pierre-du-Mesnil
Pays
Nécy
Trun
le Sap
Monnai
la Vieille-Lyre
Pierrefitte
Villers-en-Ouche
Glos-la-Ferrière
les Baux-de-B
Risle
Chambois
St. Nicolas-des-Laitiers
la Ferté-Frênel
Douche
le Bourg-St. Léonard
Exmes
Gacé
Rugles
Argentan
Haras du Pin
St. Evroult-N.-D.-du-Bois
Almenêches
Echauffour
l'Aigle
Fleuré
Nonant-le-Pin
le Merlerault
Ste. Gauburge-Ste. Colombe
Chandai
Bourth
Médavy
Planches
Crulai
Boucé
Chât. d'O
les Aspres
Verneuil-sur-Avre
Mortrée
Chailloué
Moulins-la-Marche
Avre
Randonnai
Courtomer
Sées
Soligny-la-Trappe
St. Maurice-lès-Charencey
Rouperroux
Forêt d'Ecouves
Ste. Scolasse-s.-Sarthe
Fontenai-les-Louvets
Tourouvre
Ste. Anne
Essay
Bazoches-s.-Hoëne
Marchainville
St. Denis-s.-Sarthon
le Mêle-s.-Sarthe
Feings
Sarthe
Mortagne-au-Perche
St. Mard-de-Réno
Longny-au-Perche
le Ménil-Broût
Condé-s.-Sarthe
ST. GERMAIN-DU-CORBEIS
ALENÇON
Blèves
Courgeon
le Mage
St. Paterne
St. Céneri-le-Gérei
Basse Gravelle
le Pin-la-Garenne
Moutiers-au-Perche
Neufchâtel-en-Saosnois
Boissy-Maugis
Rémalard
Béthon
Bellême
Manoir de Courboyer
Assé-le-Boisne
Mamers
Noce
Condé-sur-Huisne
St. Rémy-du-Val
la Hutte
St. Calez-en-Saosnois
Igé
Berd'huis
Courgains
St. Cosme-en-Vairais
St. Agnan-s.-Erre
Nogent-le-Rotrou
Dangeul
Marolles-les-Braults
St. Germain-de-la-Coudre
Beaumont-sur-Sarthe
Rouperroux-le-Coquet
le Theil
Souancé-au-Perche
Ségrie
St. Aignan
la Chapelle-du-Bois
St. Marceau
Courcemont
Ceton
Ballon
Bonnétable
Coudray-au-Perche
la Ferté-Bernard
Ste. Jamme-s.-Sarthe
St. Aubin-des-Coudrais
Authon-du-Perche
la Bazoge
Cormenard
St. Célerin
Tuffé
St. Ulphace
Lamnay
Perche
Gouet
la Bazoche-
la Milesse
Savigné-l'Evêque
l'Océane
Sceaux-s.-Huisne
Montmirail
St. Maixent
la Chapelle-Guillaume
Yvré-l'Evêque
Champagné
le Mans Est
Connerré
Lavaré
MANS
St. Mars-la-Brière
Thorigné-s.-Dué
Vibrave
Arville
Etival-lès-le-Mans
Anc. Abb. de l'Epau
Semur-en-Vallon
Souday
St. Agil
Allonnes
Changé
Arnage
Ruaudin
Surfonds
Bouloire
Berfay
la Chapelle-Vicomtesse
Parigné-l'Evêque
Mondoubleau
Volnay
Mulsanne
Guécélard
St. Mars-d'Outillé
Tresson
Sargé-sur-Braye
Beauchêne
St. Calais
le Temple
Yvré-le-Pôlin
le Grand Lucé
Ste. Cérotte
Epuisay
Ecommoy
St. Vincent-du-Lorouër
Savigny-sur-Braye
Danzé
Vancé
Courdemanche
Jupilles
Bessé-sur-Braye
Fortan
Azé
Mayet
Mansigné
Chât. de Courtanvaux
St. Hubert
Pontvallain

105

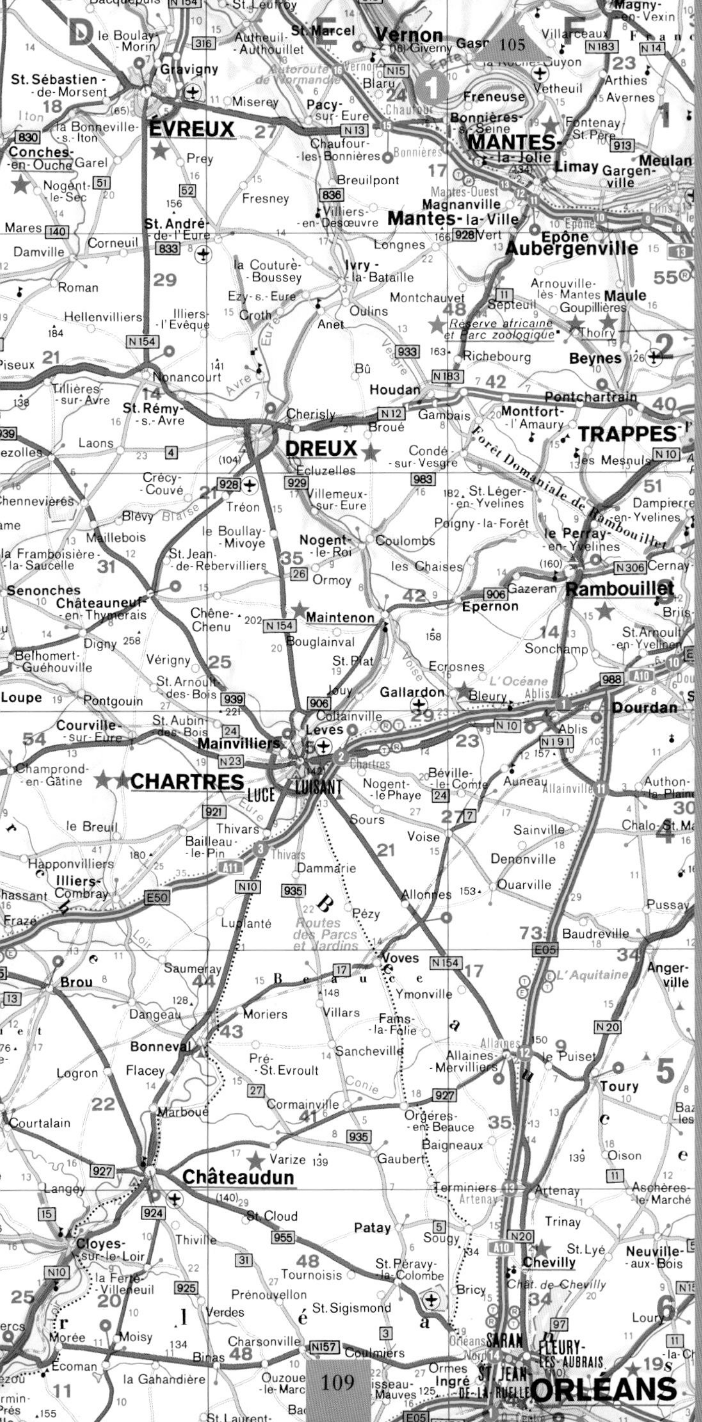
D
E
F
St. Leufroy
Magny-en-Vexin
le Boulay-Morin
Autheuil-Authouillet
St. Marcel
Vernon
Giverny
Villarceaux
Gravigny
St. Sébastien-de-Morsent
Autoroute de Normandie
Blaru
la Roche-Guyon
Arthies
Vetheuil
Miserey
Pacy-sur-Eure
Freneuse
Avernes
Iton
la Bonneville-s.-Iton
ÉVREUX
Bonnières-s.-Seine
Fontenay-St. Père
Chaufour-les-Bonnières
MANTES-la-Jolie
Conches-en-Ouche
Garel
Prey
Limay
Gargenville
Meulan
Nogent-le-Sec
Breuilpont
Fresney
Mantes-Ouest
Villiers-en-Désœuvre
Magnanville
Mantes-la-Ville
Mares
St. André-de-l'Eure
Épône
Aubergenville
Damville
Corneuil
Longnes
Vert
la Couture-Boussey
Ivry-la-Bataille
Roman
Arnouville-lès-Mantes
Maule
Ezy-s.-Eure
Montchauvet
Septeuil
Goupillières
Hellenvilliers
Illiers-l'Evêque
Croth
Oulins
Anet
Réserve africaine et Parc zoologique
Thoiry
Richebourg
Beynes
Piseux
Nonancourt
Bû
Houdan
Tillières-sur-Avre
Pontchartrain
St. Rémy-s.-Avre
Cherisly
Gambais
Montfort-l'Amaury
Broué
TRAPPES
Laons
DREUX
Condé-sur-Vesgre
les Mesnuls
Forêt Domaniale de Rambouillet
Crécy-Couvé
Écluzelles
Villemeux-sur-Eure
St. Léger-en-Yvelines
Dampierre-en-Yvelines
Tréon
Blévy
Maillebois
le Boullay-Mivoye
Nogent-le-Roi
Coulombs
Poigny-la-Forêt
le Perray-en-Yvelines
la Framboisière-la-Saucelle
St. Jean-de-Rebervilliers
Ormoy
les Chaises
Cernay
Senonches
Châteauneuf-en-Thymerais
Gazeran
Rambouillet
Épernon
Chêne-Chenu
Maintenon
Digny
Bouglainval
St. Arnoult-en-Yvelines
Belhomert-Guéhouville
Vérigny
Sonchamp
St. Piat
Ecrosnes
Bleury
L'Océane
Ablis
St. Arnoult-des-Bois
Loupe
Pontgouin
Jouy
Gallardon
Dourdan
Coltainville
Courville-sur-Eure
St. Aubin-des-Bois
Leves
Mainvilliers
Champrond-en-Gâtine
CHARTRES
LUCE
LUISANT
Béville-le-Comte
Auneau
Nogent-le-Phaye
Allainville
Authon-la-Plaine
le Breuil
Thivars
Sours
Voise
Sainville
Chalo-St. Mars
Bailleau-le-Pin
Happonvilliers
Dammarie
Denonville
Illiers-Combray
Allonnes
Quarville
Pussay
Luplanté
Pézy
Routes des Parcs et Jardins
Baudreville
Saumeray
Voves
Brou
Beauce
Ymonville
L'Aquitaine
Angerville
Dangeau
Moriers
Villars
Fains-la-Folie
Bonneval
Pré-St. Evroult
Sancheville
Allaines-Mervilliers
le Puiset
Logron
Flacey
Toury
Marboué
Cormainville
Orgères-en-Beauce
Courtalain
Baigneaux
Oison
Varize
Gaubert
Châteaudun
Langey
Terminiers
Artenay
Aschères-le-Marché
St. Cloud
Trinay
Patay
Sougy
Thiville
Cloyes-sur-le-Loir
Chevilly
Neuville-aux-Bois
St. Lyé
Tournoisis
St. Péravy-la-Colombe
la Ferté-Villeneuil
Bricy
Prénouvellon
Verdes
St. Sigismond
Loury
Morée
Moisy
Charsonville
Coulmiers
SARAN
FLEURY-LES-AUBRAIS
Binas
Écoman
la Gahandière
Ouzouer-le-Marché
Ormes
Ingré
ST. JEAN-DE-LA-RUELLE
ORLÉANS
St. Laurent

ROAD ATLAS LEGEND

le Mans-Est 4	Autobahn mit Anschlußstelle Motorway with junction
Datum, Date	Autobahn in Bau Motorway under construction
Datum, Date	Autobahn in Planung Motorway projected
R	Raststätte mit Übernachtungsmöglichkeit Roadside restaurant and hotel
R	Raststätte ohne Übernachtungsmöglichkeit Roadside restaurant
E	Erfrischungsstelle, Kiosk Snackbar, kiosk
T	Tankstelle Filling-station
	Autobahnähnliche Schnellstraße mit Anschlußstelle Dual carriage-way with motorway characteristics with junction
	Straße mit zwei getrennten Fahrbahnen Dual carriage-way
	Durchgangsstraße Thoroughfare
	Wichtige Hauptstraße Important main road
	Hauptstraße Main road
	Sonstige Straße Other road
	Bergbahn Mountain railway
	Sessellift (Auswahl) Chair-lift (selection)
	Autotransport per Bahn Transport of cars by railway
	Autofähre Car ferry
	Schiffahrtslinie Shipping route
	Landschaftlich besonders schöne Strecke Route with beautiful scenery
Routes des Crêtes	Touristenstraße Tourist route
	Straße gegen Gebühr befahrbar Toll road
	Straße für Kraftfahrzeuge gesperrt Road closed to motor traffic
	Zeitlich geregelter Verkehr Temporal regulated traffic
15%	Bedeutende Steigungen Important gradients

Kultur
Culture

★★ **PARIS** ★★ *la Alhambra*	Eine Reise wert Worth a journey
★ **TRENTO** ★ *Comburg*	Lohnt einen Umweg Worth a detour

Landschaft
Landscape

★★ **Rodos** ★★ *Fingal's cave*	Eine Reise wert Worth a journey
★ **Korab** ★ *Jaskinia raj*	Lohnt einen Umweg Worth a detour
	Besonders schöner Ausblick Important panoramic view
	Nationalpark, Naturpark National park, nature park
	Sperrgebiet Prohibited area
4807	Bergspitze mit Höhenangabe in Metern Mountain summit with height in metres
(630)	Ortshöhe Height above sea level
	Kirche Church
	Kirchenruine Church ruin
	Kloster Monastery
	Klosterruine Monastery ruin
	Schloß, Burg Palace, castle
	Schloß-, Burgruine Palace ruin, castle ruin
	Denkmal Monument
	Wasserfall Waterfall
	Höhle Cave
	Ruinenstätte Ruins
	Sonstiges Objekt Other object
	Jugendherberge Youth hostel
	Badestrand · Surfen Bathing beach · Surfing
	Tauchen · Fischen Diving · Fishing
	Verkehrsflughafen Airport
	Flugplatz Airfield

10 km

INDEX

This index lists all the main places, castles and châteaux mentioned in this guide. Numbers in bold indicate a main entry, italics a photograph.

What do you get for your money?

The unit of currency in Normandy is the French franc (abbreviated to FF) which is divided into 100 centimes. The cost of living in France is quite reasonable. Don't forget that during the holiday season, prices are at their highest, of course. However, before and after the high season, the careful holiday-maker will be able to get by quite well.

It costs around 35 FF to go 100 km on the highway. One litre of lead-free 4-star petrol costs around 6.20 FF. The cheapest place to fill up your tank is from the petrol stations at big supermarkets.

Self-caterers can wander round the popular weekly markets and they can also take advantage of the wide range of reasonably-priced, good quality goods to be found at out-of-town supermarkets.

In restaurants it is advisable to ask for the menu. From around 80 FF you should be able to get a decent meal. A good bottle of wine will set you back around 90 FF. A *café noir* after the meal will cost 10 FF. Incidentally, the famous *baguette*, that symbol of France, is subsidised by the state and will only cost you 3.50 FF.

The cost of sending a letter or a post card within the EU is 3 FF and to other European countries 3.40 FF.

FF	£	US$	Can$
1	0.09	0.15	0.22
2	0.18	0.30	0.44
3	0.27	0.45	0.66
4	0.36	0.60	0.88
5	0.45	0.75	1.10
6	0.54	0.90	1.32
7	0.63	1.05	1.54
8	0.72	1.20	1.76
9	0.81	1.35	1.98
10	0.90	1.50	2.20
15	1.35	2.25	3.30
20	1.80	3.00	4.40
25	2.25	3.75	5.50
30	2.70	4.50	6.60
40	3.60	6.00	8.80
50	4.50	7.50	11.00
75	6.75	11.25	16.50
100	9.00	15.00	22.00
250	22.50	37.50	55.00
500	45.00	75.00	110.00
1,000	90.00	150.00	220.00

Get more out of your holiday!

Use Marco Polo Language Guides to understand and be understood

- Useful phrases for every situation
- Do's and don'ts
- Complete menus
- Travelling with kids
- Over 1000 of the most important words you're ever likely to need – plus Local Tips!

These language guides are made for you!

How to say it – communication made easy!